backyard miracles

backyard miracles

Emily Billings, Karen Carlino,
Jessica Dupuy, Carrie Feder,
Jeanine Garcia, Sharon Holeman,
Joanna Jacob, Jody Calandro Kaiser,
Sandra Mizell, Brandi Redmon,
Peggy Taylor, and Lori Wilkins

CrossBooks™
A Division of LifeWay
1663 Liberty Drive
Bloomington, IN 47403
www.crossbooks.com
Phone: 1-866-879-0502

First published by CrossBooks 06/01/2012

ISBN: 978-1-4627-1657-9 (hc)
ISBN: 978-1-4627-1656-2 (e)
ISBN: 978-1-4627-1655-5 (sc)
Library of Congress Control Number: 2012906517

Cover Artwork & Interior Graphics: Praise First Media LLC
Inspired by Trading Phrases Cute Tree Giant Wall Decal
Used with permission.
praisefirstmedia.com / tradingphrases.com

Unless otherwise noted, Scripture taken from the HOLY BIBLE, NEW INTERNATIONAL VERSION ®.
Copyright © 1973, 1978, 1984 by International Bible Society. Used by permission of Zondervan. All rights reserved.
King James Version of the Holy Bible also used.

C. S. Lewis quote used with permission.
MERE CHRISTIANITY by C. S. Lewis copyright © C. S. Lewis Pte. Ltd. 1942, 1943, 1944, 1952.

TM Joyce Meyer Ministries used with permission.
joycemeyer.org

Oral Roberts quote used with permission.
Oral Roberts Evangelistic Assoc.
oralroberts.com

Author Photographs:
Sharon Holeman Photography, Praise First Media LLC
sharonholeman.com

Printed in the United States of America
This book is printed on acid-free paper.

Contents

Preface

Miracles happen every day—or so the saying goes. But is it true? The Bible says they took place, but what about in today's world? Do healings from God still occur? Are people delivered, needs met, and sins forgiven? The answer to these questions is a resounding *yes!*

April 15, 2006, was the day I rededicated my life to Christ. Since that time, I have—without question—experienced many miracles in my life. Some were large, and some were small. God has spoken to me through lightning bolts and whispers. I also believe miracles were taking place before that marvelous day in April, although I may not have been aware of them at the time.

I do know for certain of a few miracles in my life that happened prior to my day of salvation. I love this fact. It is a miracle in itself—a true sign that God loves me regardless. I can be deep in sin or living for Him, yet His love for me never changes—it is always present. What is different is my outcome—my destiny—based on my choices. His love for us is always there. His salvation has been provided for us; it is up to us to simply accept it, believe in it, and have faith in Him. The miracles in my life are wonderful reminders that He is with me, He loves me, and His Word is true.

As a tribute to these amazing occurrences, and in order to remember them, I decided to write them down. As I began, I realized I probably had enough to fill an entire book. How incredible! I started to daydream about what the book would become, and then I realized that it might be misinterpreted. Someone might think the book was about me. Thankfully, I received a better vision—a way to ensure this book would do what any miracle should do—glorify God.

I started to think about the many Christian friends I have been blessed with over the past few years. I recalled some of our conversations where they shared their stories, testimonies, and miracles.

The pages that follow are a collaboration of some of these stories. They are told by real people who have been touched by a miracle of God. Some miracles are seemingly small, some are life-changing, yet all are unforgettable.

Enjoy with me these true stories as the authors open their hearts and as we discover together that miracles really do happen every day—right in our own backyards.

Blessings.

Acknowledgments

Emily Billings
I would like to thank the staff members of the St. Louis Dream Center who were there when I did the internship, especially Pastors Jeff and Jami Allensworth, Pastor Michael Hirsch, and Sara Bowman. I would have never made it through without all of your support and love. Thank you to all the people who gave so I could go. Also, I would like to thank my husband, Craig, for being a man of his word.

Karen Carlino
God blessed me abundantly through my twenty-year friendship with Candi Jane Frezza. Her surprise visit to support me was a visible sign I had been heavy on her heart. I know she had been praying for me. Candi's love and concern began a chain reaction of life eternal.

Jessica Dupuy
For my Lord and Savior, Jesus Christ, and to my husband, Silas, my knight in shining armor.

Carrie Feder
To Jesus—I love you and thank you for saving me. To Matthew—you are my gift from God. To Memer and Daddy—thank you for always showing me unconditional love.

Jeanine Garcia
A huge thank you to all the men in my life: my husband, Peter, whose faith and wisdom inspire me daily, and my three beautiful sons, Logan, Benjamin, and Samuel—I couldn't be more proud of my three arrows. To Jesus Christ, my Savior and my Lord—apart from you, I can do nothing.

Sharon Holeman

I am blessed to be a considered child of the Most High God. All my praise goes to my heavenly Father, my blessed Savior, and my guiding Holy Spirit. To my husband, Dave—you are my mighty man of God, and I adore you. Thank you, Patrick Ross—your invitation to Dave brought us to Jesus and changed our lives forever. Michelle Puente, your beautiful heart, intent on making mine happy, is celebrated and remembered often. My greatest gratitude also goes to the eleven women who have graced me with the honor of sharing their testimonies in this book. I love you all.

Joanna Jacob

I would like to thank my Lord Jesus Christ for His amazing, unrelenting love for me, and my family—my mother, for her many "Lord have Mercy" prayers, and my brother, who never gave up on me.

Jody Calandro Kaiser

Dedicated to all eight of my sisters and brothers: C, P, P, T, M, J, C, and A. We pulled together and gave honor to God through a most difficult time.

Sandra Mizell

I want to thank my Lord Jesus for all He has done in my life. He has brought me a long way! Also, I want to thank my husband, Garlin, for his loving example and constant support in all my endeavors.

Brandi Redmon

Many people have helped me in my Christian walk—but most of all, thank you, God! My family has been very supportive, and I am grateful for every single one of you. I would also like to give my appreciation to the following people for contributing to the writing of my article: my husband, Clay; Pastor Valmon Meade; Brother Townsend; and Leonard Clements.

Peggy Taylor

Praise God, from whom all blessings flow. Thanks to my husband and best friend, Wesley, and to my family for their love and support.

Lori Wilkins

To all those who spoke the truth in love—I am forever grateful.

In addition

Sincere thanks goes to the following people for their help in making this book become a reality: Casey Bombacie, Alexis Carrasquel, Hannah and Warren Couvillion, Patrice Couvillion, John Coxe, Kerry Duplessis, Brittany Howard, Rhonda Innis, Janelle and Dennis Hart, Kim and David Holeman Sr., Susan Jen, Jay Kaiser, Mitch Lovett, Deborah Lynne, Diane and Bob Moulds, Cyndi Roberts, Stephanie Shaffett, Larry Stockstill, and Tammy Tokosh.

The Road to Forgiveness

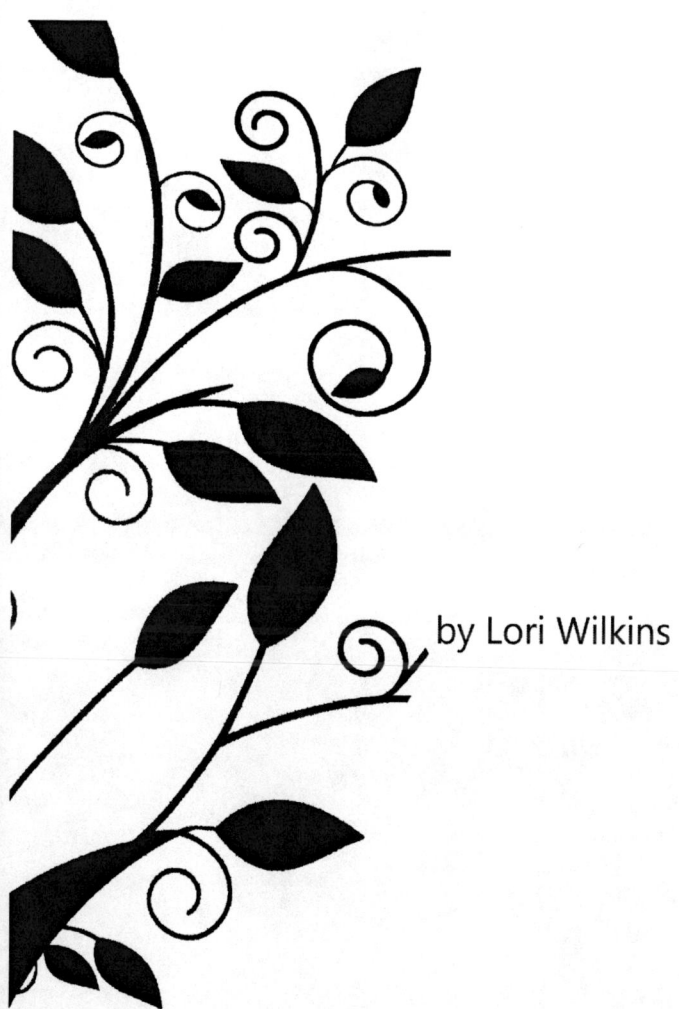

by Lori Wilkins

Let me start by saying it is an honor to be a part of this project. I know and love many of the women whose testimonies are written in this book. The way I have witnessed them serve the Lord with their time and talent is amazing to me. I am not sure how I became included in this group, but I know the Lord always has a purpose and a plan. I also know there is great power in the sharing of one's personal testimony. Hearing a great pastor, speaker, or friend tell the intimate details of his or her life, successes and struggles, joys and sorrows; what God has taught and brought him or her through, is one of the things that has helped me the most over the years.

Revelation 12:11 says, *"They overcame him by the blood of the Lamb and by the word of their testimony."*

Hearing the stories of others has been a major part of my healing process, though many of the people will never know how much they have helped me until I can tell them, one day, in heaven.

Though I am grateful for the opportunity to serve the Lord in this way, it has been a much more difficult task than I ever imagined. Almost daily, I have the opportunity to talk with women about the issues of life. Talking with people is easy for me, like drinking water or breathing, but writing is hard. I have a new found respect for the authors of all the books I have read throughout the years. That being said, here is my story.

I was born in Florida and moved to coastal Georgia at about four years of age. My mom and dad were having some sort of trouble, so we moved in with my grandmother in her big, two-story house on Union Street. I have two brothers and one sister, plus two half-sisters whom we welcomed as often as they could visit. Between us all, I am sure we turned Grandma's formerly quiet nest upside down. One of us dropped her little dog all the way from the top of the stairs. Another time I accidentally slammed Grandma's finger in the trunk. I nearly passed out as she said "Darn nation." Those were the days when grownups didn't use curse words.

My parents were both raised in homes with Christian beliefs, but like all families, imperfections existed. My parents always made sure we went to church—even on the Sundays they didn't. I am probably most grateful for that. They taught us that all people deserve respect and that Jesus is our Savior and closest friend. They sent us to Vacation Bible School, Sunday school, and church camp. My mom walked with me down the aisle of our church when I was twelve. I asked Jesus into my heart and then cried all the way home in the car.

Eventually, we moved out from Grandma's and got a place of our own. I have many happy memories from my childhood. A lot of it was normal— laughing, fussing and fighting with brothers and sisters, cooking, and eating. My dad was the best; I loved it when he cooked.

Some of my fondest memories of Mom were times spent at the beach. We only lived a few minutes away, and we went often. She would cover us with sand; we'd laugh and play all day. She was a great mom.

Although my parents were fun and loving, we were oftentimes a family in crisis, dealing with problems that were rather intense. I think I was about six or seven when Mom was diagnosed with a chronic mental illness. She was a registered nurse by occupation and one of the most intelligent people I had ever known. She was hard-working and dedicated. I went to work with her occasionally, admiring the loving care she gave her patients. She explained to them the importance of taking their medicine, but every so often, she would stop taking her own. She wouldn't be able to sleep for several days and before long would wind up in the hospital. As a child, I didn't understand her extreme mood swings or the resulting drama that sometimes ensued as a result of the illness that tormented her mind. Mom's behavior was hard for me to comprehend, yet I ached for the hearts of my younger siblings.

During the times Mom was hospitalized, we kids would stay home with Dad or a sitter or sometimes have an extended visit with my aunt or grandmother. When Mom came home, she would be good for about a year, and the whole thing would start all over again.

I'm sure the happenings at our house were the topic of dinner table conversations around the neighborhood. This, I'm certain, was especially true on the days an ambulance or police car would make an appearance in our driveway. Once I overheard a neighbor comment about how intelligent a woman my mom was; they wondered how this could be happening. I wondered the same thing.

I remember coming home from school one day. My mom was in the hospital, and my dad was on his bed, sobbing. He looked up at me and said, "I wish I was Superman, but I'm not." I will never forget that day. It broke my heart, and it made me realize that he was hurting, too.

Dad handled things the best he could, but he was ill, too. He struggled with alcohol. He never seemed drunk. His speech was never slurred, and he never staggered. He always seemed in control. In fact, he was quite funny—a clown who liked to make us laugh. My mom, however, didn't find it humorous when he would leave for bread and come back two days later, grocery sack in hand.

The cycle of illness and related troubles continued until one day, my dad told us we were moving from the beautiful Golden Isles of Georgia to Arkansas, where his parents lived. He had gotten a good job there. The town was small, with a population of less than five thousand, one grocery store, and worst of all, no beach. I was fourteen.

Up until then, I felt I had been fairly patient with the events that had been taking place in my family, but now they were pushing it! They were telling me that after all I had been through, we were moving away from my home, my ocean, and my support system. My mom's family had been a huge part of our lives growing up, and the thought of leaving them literally made me sick. I especially hated to leave my cousin. I cherished her; she was older than me and spent quite a bit of time with us. She chose to be with us when she could have been doing other things—things that young people her age were doing. Now this extended family, which served as a backup plan if I ever needed help, would be hundreds of miles away. What would I do?

What I did was get mad, and things got worse. One day, after the move, I came home from school and walked into chaos. All the anger, frustration, and fear that had been bottled up in me for so long came out. I begged my parents to let me go back to Georgia and live with my grandmother. I made my parents' lives miserable. They actually considered granting my request but decided I should stay with them. How they put up with me, I don't know. My behavior was horrible.

I was fifteen when my mom and dad divorced. My sister and I went to live with my mom across town. The boys stayed with Dad, and things between us got tangled. I was angry with my dad. I was frustrated with my mom, because she wouldn't stay on her medication. I was just plain mad. I decided to save up enough money to go back to Georgia and live with my grandmother. I was going to take control of my life. I planned to eventually get my own place and live in peace, by myself, and no one was going to throw dishes, or fuss and fight, or tell me when I had to move.

Time passed, but I got stuck. Have you ever known someone who was full of resentment and bitterness yet couldn't see it? No one can help that person, and that person was me. It was like everything caught up with me at once, and I got stuck. I just couldn't sort it out in my mind.

I was now an adult and totally relying on my own strength. I was so far away from God, I didn't know if I was coming or going. The only prayer I prayed was, "God help me," but I didn't listen for His response. I wanted to be left alone, but I was lonely. I tried to find love and acceptance in relationships; it didn't work. I tried to drink alcohol, but that didn't work either. I moved to another town, went back to school, and got a degree in a field I had absolutely no interest in. No matter what I did or which way I turned, I made a bigger mess of my life.

One day a married couple, whom I worked with, confronted me. They looked me in the eye and lovingly said, "What are you doing, Lori?" They were two Christians whom I greatly admired. I felt as if they were holding up a mirror, and for the first time, I realized how lost I really was. I started attending their church and spent many nights on their sofa next to the fireplace, being mentored by a godly husband and wife who were walking the walk. My life started to change, but I was still holding on to unforgiveness—mainly toward my parents.

Once again, I moved, and once again, I met some wonderful people who were patient and kind and listened to me. Every sermon I heard seemed to be on unforgiveness. On the radio, I heard, "Our topic today is unforgiveness." I attended a support group for families that dealt with some of the issues mine had, and what did they talk about? You guessed it: learning to forgive.

A lady named Alice, a Christian, was at the support group, and she really made a difference in my life. Alice told me I couldn't do what I needed to do without God's help. Soon afterward, I had an experience I will never forget as long as I live.

While at home one evening, distraught, I threw myself on the floor face-down and cried out to God. "I need your help, Lord! I am going to lose it if you don't help me. I have no peace, and if you will help me, please do it now, because I feel like I'm going to die." Silently, I got up off the floor and lay on the couch. All of a sudden, I felt like someone covered me with a blanket of love. I couldn't move, but I didn't want to move. I knew the Lord heard my cry and had come to give me peace—to let me know I was going to be okay.

Since then, I have felt the presence of the Lord many times, but never as strong as that night. That night was a turning point in my life. I told the Lord I was sorry for my attitude, my sin, the way I had been disrespectful to my parents, running from Him, and the awful way I had treated the people I really loved. I poured my heart out to Him in a way I never had before, and He was right there beside me.

I believe an honest, desperate cry to Jesus will always be heard and answered. Revelation 3:20 says, *"Here I am! I stand at the door and knock. If anyone hears my voice and opens the door, I will come in and eat with him, and he with me."*

Salvation is a miracle. It is an event. You should be able to remember when it happened to you. Restoration is a process. It happens over a lifetime. My experience on the couch was twenty-two years ago. Restoration is still happening in my life. It comes with revelation, which comes from the Word of God.

The Bible was written for you and me. It is food for our souls, and we need to read it every day, just like we eat daily. Memorizing Scripture can save your life. The Word will give you a firm foundation to stand on when the rest of the world seems to be crumbling around you.

My favorite Scripture—the one that keeps me going—is Psalm 31:15: *"My times are in your hands."* This reminds me I am not in control, but Jesus is.

I believe forgiveness is the single most important thing you can allow God to teach you. If you don't, your unwillingness to forgive is like a wall separating you from the Lord. The Holy Spirit will teach you, but you have to take the first step and be willing to do it—to let it all go.

In Corrie ten Boom's book *The Hiding Place,* the author had an amazing experience with forgiveness. She was taken to a concentration camp for hiding Jews in Nazi Germany, and her father died ten days after their arrival. Corrie then had to watch people be cruel to her sister, who also eventually died in the camp. Years after these horrible experiences, she wrote in her next book, *Tramp for the Lord,* about forgiveness and how it helped people rebuild their lives. Her powerful words stuck with me.

I had been my own worst enemy. My horrible attitude poisoned everything I did. When I read about Corrie ten Boom, I realized just how blessed I was. Her story helped me get over myself. She forgave the prison guards who were so cruel to her and her family. She shook their hands and prayed with them. If she could forgive, then I could. And I did—with God's help. I also asked my family to forgive me. What might have been the hardest part was forgiving myself. Forgiveness is important if you want to move forward and not stay stuck in mistakes of the past.

"Be kind and compassionate to one another, forgiving each other, just as Christ God forgave you" (Ephesians 4:32).

My road forward included finding a wonderful, Bible-based church and a strong Christian support network called a life group. The love and friendship of this group of ladies was vital to my spiritual growth. Sometimes I would walk in, say hello, and with no other information, the group members could tell I needed extra attention. Mama eyes would peer from over the top of reading glasses, looking at my face, but seeing straight into my heart. They knew me so well that they could read my face—it's the same thing as being transparent. "How are you, Ms. Lori?"

"Fine," I would say. But before the evening was over, the group's members would lay hands on me in prayer, and that was okay. I never tried to lie to them if something was bothering me; rather, I just put it on the table. The group was a place of safety, and I knew I was accountable to ladies who had my best interest at heart. I could trust them with the truth. We laughed, cried, and let it all hang out. Then we prayed about everything.

"Therefore confess your sins to each other and pray for each other so that you may be healed. The prayer of a righteous man is powerful and effective" (James 5:16).

These ladies brought much joy to my life, and I gave them full permission to ask me the same question I was asked many years ago: "What are you doing, Lori?"

Once I got myself out of the way and let the Lord be the king of my life, I was transformed, and my relationships were restored. My dad and I enjoy the closest relationship we have ever had. He has recovered from a lot of his wounds, been sober for many years, and is an active part of his church. My mom is in heaven, completely healed, and I'll see her one day.

As for me, I am a functioning part of the body of Christ. I still belong to a wonderful church as well as to my cherished life group. I enjoy the continued fellowship and spiritual growth I share with these ladies whom I love very much. I have a heart for children and volunteer with the youth program. I long to share the safety, love, and forgiveness that Christ has given me with others. I still sometimes ask myself, "What are you doing, Lori?" and tend to gauge my spiritual thermometer by how frequently I pray for a stranger in the grocery store.

The quiet home I always wanted is now a reality, complete with a husband who is peaceful and calm. Every day as I wake up, I lie on my bed and thank the Lord for all He has done for me. I thank Him for what He has done and for what He continues to do. In those still moments of the morning, sometimes I can almost sense that God is smiling; happy I thought of Him first and ready to cover me in the blanket of love He so graciously provides.

"Praise be to the Lord, who has given rest to his people ... Not one word has failed of all the good promises he gave" (1 Kings 8:56).

The Straightened Path

by Karen Carlino

In March of 2010, I was asked to do a spur-of-the-moment medical exam on an individual for a major insurance company. I agreed, not knowing this appointment would be unlike any other.

My training in paramedical services had led me into a freelance career of doing physicals for individuals who were applying for new insurance policies. I loved my job, the flexible part-time schedule, and all the people I met along the way.

When the day arrived, I approached the cream-colored brick house, rang the doorbell, and waited. The house was similar to other homes in the neighborhood: typical style and size, with a neatly trimmed lawn. While each case is unique and each client special in his or her own way, with over twenty-five years of appointments behind me, I expected this visit to be routine. When the door opened, however, a miracle began.

My client, still a stranger to me, greeted me with a friendly hello and a Scripture quotation. A smile spread across my face as I asked, "What kind of work do you do?" He said he was retired from the post office but served as a pastor. He was tall, dark, and handsome—a striking black man in his fifties with gray hair. He had an aura of peace and strength about him. Our conversation flowed easily as we discussed the weather, required business talk, and of course, our faith. Following the exam, as Pastor Lee walked me out to my car, he mentioned being disappointed his wife had not been home. He thought she would have enjoyed meeting me.

"Where is she today?" I asked.

His reply was simply, "Dialysis." I inquired if she was registered on a transplant list, and he said she was, through Tulane Medical Center in New Orleans. It had been almost a year, and there had not been any matches. But they continued to pray and trust God.

As he explained the trial they were facing, my mind raced. Memories came flooding in of the hospital room I had been in several years prior. I spent too long in that room, but during that time, I experienced divine intervention in a very personal way. I was saved from almost certain death and suffered a fractured neck and head injury from a car accident in 2003. I identified with the uncertainty my client was feeling.

The physical pain from my injuries had been tough, but the emotional pain was nearly unbearable. The accident that had broken my body also took the life of my best friend.

Candi had been my closest friend the majority of my life. We met at the beginning of high school and were, at the time, seemingly inseparable. We shared everything from teenage heartaches to trips to the mall, homework study sessions, and long, fun-filled summers. She was always there for me. I could always count on Candi.

Though many years had passed and we each were married with our own lives, she remained my cherished companion. The fact that she was living in Jackson, Mississippi – over 150 miles away from my home in Baton Rouge, Louisiana—was of no matter. She drove in and surprised me when I needed her the most. The divorce I went through had taken its toll, and Candi came to spend time with me, reassure me, and make me laugh. She could always make me laugh.

Candi was beautiful. Even after the passage of countless days and trials of everyday life, she remained captivating. Her golden brown hair and sparkling eyes were refreshing to my shattered state; her words were soothing and kind. I distinctly remember her saying, with her slow southern accent, "I know in my heart Karen will be fine."

Candi accompanied me out the night of the accident in an effort to cheer me up. I had confided in another faithful friend, alcohol, and thus, Candi was driving us home. The truck that hit us came fast from out of the darkness. The sound of screeching tires, the feeling of the intense crash, the sight of flying debris, and an unimaginable amount of blood along with the smell of burnt rubber and heat overwhelmed me. It was horrible and unbelievable. Candi was gone.

At the time, I was not saved; I did not have a personal relationship with the Lord, yet He spared my life. Those days in the hospital and many following were some of the hardest I have known. I grieved. I cried. I questioned everything. My path, however, led to the best place possible—a place that was new and comforting to me. I fell into the arms of Jesus. I began to learn of His great love for me and what He had done for me on the cross. My life was forever changed.

Since that time, I longed to give back. My heart's desire became for God to use me. I prayed, "If there is anything I can do for someone else—an encouraging word, a smile, a need to fill—please let me."

My thoughts came back to the moment I was in, seven years later, standing with Pastor Lee outside his home on a lovely spring day. This seemed like the perfect opportunity to give back.

Unbeknownst to Pastor Lee, I began the process to see if I would be an acceptable match. I made numerous trips to Tulane, about an hour away, undergoing various medical tests. My desire to donate my kidney to his wife, Gloria—a woman I had not yet met—grew stronger every day. Being in the medical profession, however, I knew the odds of us being a match were not good, so to avoid creating false hope, I said nothing.

One of my favorite Scriptures is in Proverbs. I have it taped to my mirror and read it every day. It says, *"Trust in the Lord with all your heart and lean not on your own understanding; in all your ways acknowledge him, and he will make your paths straight"* (Proverbs 3:5–6). I believe that is indeed what the Lord did the morning I met Pastor Lee.

The day I had been anticipating finally arrived. I received a telephone call from the transplant coordinator at Tulane. She said I had passed the medical tests, and our blood types were even the same—not a requirement, but a wonderful surprise. Our match appeared to be a good one. The coordinator saw no reason to delay the scheduling of the surgery. My heart leapt with joy. I knew this was something only the Lord could have arranged!

I brought my friend, Tanya, with me to the restaurant where I planned to share the results of my test. We sat across the table from Pastor Lee and his wife, Gloria, as I silently prayed for confirmation. It came at the end of the meal when Gloria—a short black woman with shoulder-length hair and a wonderfully sweet smile—pulled a small red prayer book out from her purse and laid it on the table. It was a gift for me. Tanya squirmed with delight. It was the same prayer book she had at home—one with very special meaning. As Tanya and I got into my car, she could hardly contain herself. This was meant to be.

The transplant was done on October 26 and could not have gone more beautifully. The surgeons said several times that they had never seen anything like it—the blood work, kidney function, and recovery all happening so smoothly.

After the surgery, my first visitor was Pastor Lee. He wanted to thank me again for giving his wife her life back. We shared a short conversation and exchanged smiles, knowing our meeting that fateful morning in March had been carefully pre-arranged by a powerful, loving God.

Gloria, who had been receiving dialysis when I first met her husband, had amazingly been telling everyone at her appointment that day, "The Lord has a kidney with my name on it." At the time, she received laughs, but in the fall, she received her miracle.

Pastor Lee and I shared a moment of silence, and as I gazed out the hospital room window, much to my delight, I saw a rainbow. It was magnificent, stretching over the entire city. The colors were almost translucent, yet vibrant in the shades of sunlight. In the book of Genesis, the rainbow represented God's promise. For me that day, it felt like the fulfillment of one—a sign of God's unwavering love.

I was encouraged with cards, calls, and prayers from family, friends, and everyone on staff at my contract office, as well as fellow examiners. Within two weeks of the surgery, I was back at work. My procedure was done laparoscopically, and the recovery was quite rapid.

My relationship with Pastor Lee and Gloria is, of course, a special one. And I love hearing Gloria share her testimony; it always bring a smile to my face and joy to my heart. She recently shared with her church, "I was praying for a kidney, and no one was a match. One morning, when

I wasn't even home, my kidney came walking right up to my front door and rang the bell! That's how I know it was God."

My excitement about donating an organ to a stranger may seem odd to some, but it was a blessing for me. I was honored to give back in the name of Jesus—the one who gave His life for me. He gave us everything. I only gave a kidney.

"I have been crucified with Christ and I no longer live, but Christ lives in me. The life I live in the body, I live by faith in the Son of God, who loved me and gave himself for me" (Galatians 2:20).

Lightning Bolts and Whispers

by Sharon Holeman

It was the spring of 1991. I was a senior in college, studying business management and marketing. I lived with my twin sister and our two cats in a large, two-bedroom, two-bathroom apartment. My sister and I paid our way through college, so both of us had full-time jobs or multiple part-time jobs. We were busy and independent, yet we still enjoyed the party life many people our age were living.

My sister and I had just returned from a spring break trip to California. We drove non-stop with two of our girlfriends from San Antonio to the Los Angeles area. We took shifts in pairs of two—my twin and I were at the helm during the first four-hour leg, and our two friends took the next shift. We alternated until we made it to the west coast, even driving overnight through a snow storm in New Mexico.

Once in California, we stayed with a friend of one of the girls on the trip. We visited the beach, restaurants, nightclubs, and of course, the famed local theme parks. It was a great vacation in many ways. But I had a secret. It was a terrible secret I thought no one would understand, so I kept it to myself.

I had been attacked just prior to leaving for the trip. Not physically attacked—rather, it was an attack one rarely hears of. It was unfamiliar and seemed to come out of nowhere, yet it was the most devastating deception I could ever imagine.

I was packing for the trip in my room at the apartment. My sister and I had taken our cats to the veterinary office to be boarded for the week. I was on the floor, gathering up the Sunday newspaper, which lay beside my bed. As I gathered the paper, I flipped through it, landing on a full-page advertisement. It was a red and black graphic for a clothing store. As I glanced at the page, I heard a voice in my head say, "Give me your soul. Just say yes."

I was horrified! I thought to myself, *No.* The voice returned, with the same prompting. "Just say yes." I repeated my response. *No.* The voice came again with more urgency and fed the word over and over inside my head: "Yes. Yes. Yes."

I spoke aloud this time. "No." More firmly the second time, I said, "No." Finally, I shouted, "No!"

My sister, packing in her room, asked loudly, "Are you okay? I thought you were talking to the cats at first, but they aren't here."

The silent battle ended, broken by her words. "I'm fine," I replied. I quickly closed the newspaper, gathered it, and rushed to the large kitchen trash can. I didn't speak of what happened. I was thrown by it. What had happened? I had been attacked by an enemy that was not flesh and blood. I had been blindsided and was unprepared. I was shaken and afraid.

"For our struggle is not against flesh and blood, but against the rulers, against the authorities, against the powers of this dark world and against the spiritual forces of evil in the heavenly realms" (Ephesians 6:12).

The attack rocked my false sense of security. When I was awake, I was tormented by the thought I was going to hell. My heart shouted, *No!* I fell to my knees. I cried in desperation. I felt like I had jumped into an endless black hole, with certain death and never-ending torment awaiting me. There was no escape.

I made it through my spring break vacation by sleeping and keeping my mind occupied. The few times things were quiet, my thoughts would rip apart my insides. I ached.

Upon return to college, work, and a regular schedule, my life was much of the same. I knew my only help would come from God. I didn't know what else to do, so I started to read my Bible each night before bed. I started with the first chapter, Genesis, and read straight through. I didn't understand much of it. The names were hard to pronounce, and many of the countries were places that no longer existed. I wasn't sure how it was helping, but I knew God was my only hope.

"Jesus answered, 'I am the way and the truth and the life. No one comes to the Father except through me'" (John 14:6).

One evening, after I had done my nightly reading, I felt like I should continue, so I did. I read a little more but still did not feel a connection or find any relevance to my life. I looked around my room. It was small and clean. My bed was flanked by a dresser on one side and a fold-out modern chair on the other. This fold-out chair had been my bed in high school. I loved it. It was pale yellow in color and just plain fun.

Another treasured item was a wooden Jesus fish. It was from the Methodist church my mom brought us to for a few years during my middle school days. One year, during a church bazaar, there was a man selling hand-made wooden items at his booth. I instantly fell in love with the Jesus fish, and my sweet mother bought it for me. It was simple, yet powerful. The fish sat on the middle portion of the one tall, thin window in my room. It was behind the blinds, not visible inside the spectrum of my room. If I wanted to see it, I had to raise the blinds and let in the light, and then I could see the Jesus fish. Ironically, this signified the place I had given the Lord in my life.

I looked back at my Bible and struggled to read more. My heart wasn't in it. I decided I was done for the night. As I closed my Bible, I had a very distinctive, yet nonchalant thought, *Oh well, if God wants me to keep reading, He'll tell me.*

At the very millisecond that thought finished in my mind—the room shook. Boom! Crash! Lightning struck outside, and thunder boomed. It shook my entire room. My wooden Jesus fish fell out of the window and onto the floor. I flew off the bed and huddled in the corner of my room, as far away from the window as possible. I was shaking, afraid to move. God had just spoken to me.

After a few moments, I mustered enough courage to crawl across the hall and into my sister's room. I told her what happened; certain she too would know God had spoken. She sleepily said it was nothing and rolled over.

I crawled back to my room. She was wrong. God had been in this place. God spoke to me. There was no denying it. After a few minutes of shaking in disbelief on the carpet, I picked up my Jesus fish and placed it back in the window, unharmed. I tucked myself tightly underneath the covers on my bed and began to read my Bible again. I stayed awake that night as long as I could, which I believe was around 3:00 in the morning. I was afraid to stop reading. God was watching me. He was listening to me. He could hear my thoughts. Most amazingly of all, though, He was responding.

This was not coincidence. There was nothing haphazard about the timing of the lightning bolt or the fact the only thing that moved in my room was the representation of Jesus.

"You were shown these things so that you might know that the Lord is God; besides him there is no other" (Deuteronomy 4:35).

I do not remember if it rained that night, but I am certain there were no other room-shaking thunder claps or lightning strikes. And I know I desperately needed God during that time of my life. I needed to know He still loved me and that all hope was not lost. Lovingly, in that moment, God was there. His message to me was one I will keep with me all the days of my life: God is real. God is with us. God loves us and wants us to read the Word—His Word.

"All Scripture is God-breathed..." (2 Timothy 3:16).

As time passed, I began to feel more secure—more normal again. I continued reading my Bible every night, although I rarely prayed. I started to slip back into the ways of the world. The moment I had experienced, so clearly of God, was left to memory as I grew comfortable, complacent, and caught up in life. Eventually, I stopped reading altogether.

The Old Testament is filled with stories of God's chosen people, the Israelites, and their foolish actions. When we read of their awesome experiences with God—the miracles they saw, many in which the people actually took part—we often shake our heads at their response. They hear from God. They follow Him for a period of time. They forget about the wonderful things He has done for them. They turn away from God only to find themselves once again in a bad situation. How silly.

God parted the Red Sea so the Israelites could safely cross ahead of their pursuing enemies—what a miracle! God delivered the Israelites out of the bondage of slavery and from the hands of the Egyptians through marvelous signs and wonders. God rained down a sweet, bread-like substance, called manna, out of the sky for them to eat. Yet the Israelites ended up wandering around the dessert for forty years due to their unfaithfulness.

I, too, was silly and foolish. I was just like the Israelites. I forgot. I got caught up in my world—my needs and desires. I stopped seeking the Lord, stopped reading my Bible, and was unfaithful to Him.

GROWING UP

As a child, I loved God. I had a good relationship with Him. I talked to Him every night. I wanted to be close—to know more. I don't remember going to church, except for a couple of years in middle school, but as a younger child, I loved the Lord. My mother is a believer, so I asked her questions. She taught me the Lord's Prayer, answered my questions, and went with me to buy my first Bible. She was my first spiritual teacher, and I will always love her for those early lessons and encouragement to build a relationship with our heavenly Father.

My prayer life was strong and consistent as I grew through elementary school. But sadly, as the pressures of middle school began to encroach, I became distracted by my insecurities. The years we were in church were the same years I began to walk away from the Lord. I had other priorities. I longed to be popular, be a cheerleader, and become a member of the in-crowd. I failed. My insecurities mounted, and my tendencies to be quiet transformed into a near shutdown. I was miserable, and it was completely a result of my own shortcomings and fears.

High school was a completely different experience. At the end of my ninth grade year, I was eligible to try out for our school's dance team. I made the team, and it was as if overnight everything changed. My self-confidence skyrocketed. The prestige that came with being on the award-winning squad was exciting. I believe, however, it was the attention of the boys I enjoyed most. The next three years were filled with fun, laughter, friendships, group dates, and lots of flirting.

Alcohol entered my world around my junior year. I became a party girl. Through it all, I always thought I was a good person. Despite my fun-loving nature, I still had an air of innocence within me. I would cling to that, and it made me feel safe. It made me invincible.

I had stopped praying. I stopped talking to God. I practically forgot about Him. I was self-absorbed. Yet throughout it all, there was an optimism inside of me that never left—my gift from Him, I suppose. The goodness and security in my heart were things I took for granted. I didn't realize how precious they were. I didn't realize they were Him. I buried them inside and allowed myself to get swept away in the ways of the world.

THE MIRACLE OF THE MOMENT

Eleven years after my lightning bolt experience on March 15, 1991, I had progressed further down the passageways of life, yet I found nothing. By the summer of 2002, I had graduated from college, moved to Austin, moved to Houston, studied graphic design in art school, run a marathon, traveled to London and Paris, and become a pretty good country western dancer. I found myself happy. I had a great job at a fine art company. I had just gotten back from Europe. I was in the best shape of my life, running six miles several times a week. I was happy, yet I was still searching.

And then there was a moment. It was just a moment—a fragment of time that passed as quickly as every other moment. The difference was it was unlike any I had ever experienced. It was an unspoken message that would change my life forever. It was another word from God, although I didn't understand it at the time. As C. S. Lewis said, "When the most important things in our life happen we quite often do not know, at the moment, what is going on."

It was early July and I planned to spend the Independence Day holiday with my good friend Tonya. She had invited me to go out with her and her boyfriend. They were bringing a friend whom they had pre-selected for me. He was very nice, but not a match. He was dressed in a preppy style and seemed to have an air of maturity about him—so not my type. We watched fireworks atop a building, although the night seemed rather dull due to the lack of sparks between me and my so-called date.

A couple of days later I packed and headed out on a three hour road-trip to San Antonio. The agenda was slated for visits with friends and family.

One of my main stops was Michelle's apartment. Michelle and I had become friends during college while working together. I was her boss, but she became one of my dearest friends.

When I arrived at Michelle's, I was tired and did not really feel like going out, but I didn't tell her. She was happy to see me and excited to be able to spend some time together. I changed clothes in her bathroom and decided to make the best of it. I was looking forward to visiting with Michelle, and if it was in a bar, that was fine.

I put on my favorite pair of jeans—dark blue suede-like material with no back pockets—a dressy blue patterned halter top, and black boots. I wore a beaded blue wire necklace with matching earrings.

It was a group of girls that night—me, Michelle, and three others. I didn't know some of the other girls very well, but large groups are always fun when you are tackling the adventures of nightlife. We headed to a dance pub ornamented in an Irish style decor. It was a brand-new location, and the girls wanted to check it out.

The pub was large and crowded. The main room had long, picnic-style tables stretching the length of the floor. The bar was to the left, with the stage and dance floor directly in front of the long tables. A side room to the left, behind the bar, housed pool tables, booths, and small, tall round tables for more intimate conversations.

We walked in and immediately hit the bar for drinks. For some strange reason, it is uncomfortable to be inside a bar and not holding a drink.

We made a lap around the entire pub to explore the facility and take in the scenery. We ended up finding a spot to stand and visit in the smaller room.

We were happily talking amongst ourselves. A few fellows at the nearby table began to converse with us, so I lingered and chatted. I wasn't attracted to any of them but enjoyed the talk just the same. After several minutes had passed, Michelle came over and excused me from the distraction. Back at the group, the others asked why I was talking to those guys—after all, they were not attractive. I shrugged my shoulders and said, "I don't know; we were just talking."

Michelle said, "She's too nice to be mean." Michelle and I then ventured off on our own for a sight-seeing lap and another trip to the bar. There was a tall, dark, and handsome guy at the bar, but he did not return my silent, lingering glance, so I felt no need to stay in the area. Michelle also saw no interesting prospects.

As we were walking near the bar, alongside the picnic tables, a blur of cuteness caught my attention. He was tall, dark, and handsome; young-looking; and wore a bit of a smile. He rushed through the crowd. He moved so quickly that I didn't even have time to elbow Michelle and tell her to look at the cute boy. Like a flash, he was gone.

Michelle and I made our way around the pub and back to the other three girls, who were still in the small side room. The band had started playing again after a break, and the girls wanted to dance. The five of us made our way to the large room and to the front corner of the stage. They began to dance together, enjoying the rock music the band was playing. Michelle and I chose not to dance, but stayed up front, close to our friends.

I am not one to normally notice the band, but as we stood at the corner of the stage and the dance floor, I looked up. Much to my delight, there he was—the cute guy I had seen breezing through the pub a few minutes earlier. "Oh my gosh," I said aloud.

Michelle saw that I was looking at the lively bass player near the end of the stage and asked, "Do you know him?"

"No," I replied, unable to take my eyes off of him. "But I saw him earlier and thought he was cute."

He wore steel-toe boots, flared blue jeans, and a seventies-style yellow and orange polyester long-sleeved shirt. His dark hair was greased back, and he had a marvelously chiseled jaw line. He moved back and forth, intensely playing his guitar, unaware we were watching. I began to tell Michelle about my date from July fourth—the preppy man with the long shorts, polo shirt, and penny loafers who did not suit me at all. But this—this was what I liked. I liked the way he was dressed, the way he looked, and the obvious joy he showed as he played music. He didn't seem too serious or mature; he just seemed to be having fun.

I was still looking at him as I finished my statements of approval when it happened—the miraculous moment that would change my life forever. He looked at me. He looked directly at me and smiled. I was mesmerized. I hadn't been able to take my eyes off him since I first saw him on the stage, but now that he was looking directly at me, it was as if everything stopped. It was one of those magic moments from the movies. It was just me and him. Time was still. There were no other people in the room. There was no sound. It was just me and him—and a powerful connection.

I was awoken out of the moment by Michelle's elbow to my arm. "He's smiling at you!" she said. I instantly blushed and turned away. He had been looking at me and smiling. Time had stopped, although in reality, just a moment had passed. But it was a moment that was unlike any I had ever known. It was something I thought only happened in movies—not in real life and not to two people. But it did.

The handsome bass player on the stage that night soon became my husband. He was mesmerized in the moment too. The moment happened for him as well—time stood still, and nothing else was there except for me.

Looking back, we now believe that moment happened because God wanted to make sure we noticed each other. We have also come to realize there was someone else in the moment besides my husband and myself—God.

Even when I was living in sin—even when I was disobedient and ungrateful—God's amazing love for me continued.

"But God demonstrates his own love for us in this: While we were still sinners, Christ died for us" (Romans 5:8).

WHISPERS

Our journey as husband and wife began one day shy of a year after the night we met. We married in my husband's hometown of Baton Rouge, Louisiana. After a honeymoon and the time it took to purchase a small, two-room cabin on the lake just outside of town, we were officially living as a young married couple.

The first two and a half years of marriage were less than ideal. We quickly ran out of money and had trouble finding work. Our home was filled with floodwaters and fights. Dave was angry. I was jealous. Dave was selfish. I was prideful. We were miserable, and we were broken. I felt more alone than I had ever felt in my entire life.

Talks of leaving were not uncommon, but we always went back to that moment on the night we met—our God moment. In fact, that moment in the bar kept us together. We were living in the world, deep in the struggles of life—but we had that moment. We didn't understand it, but we knew for whatever reason, God had put us together. And despite all the times we hurt each other, our love remained strong. We stayed together.

One day, out of the blue, Dave asked if I wanted to go to church with him. I was surprised and happily agreed. We tried a handful of churches, but I didn't feel at home in any of them. I didn't feel any different.

Our friend, Pat, was a musician like Dave. He had invited Dave to play Christian rock music. That is why Dave had wanted to go to church—

so he could play music again. The music and his growing relationship with the Lord seemed to instantly revive him.

There were weeks Dave went to church without me. I hadn't found any place where I was comfortable. Many Sundays, I didn't want to go through the motions: get dressed up, go feel uncomfortable, and walk away feeling as empty as I had before I walked through the doors. But Dave didn't give up on me. He continued to invite me and tried different churches with me until we found one I liked.

When we did, I knew instantly. It had a great energy and a pastor who spoke to me through teachings that I absorbed like a sponge. It was all different. I actually looked forward to going to church. I began to change.

One weekday, while washing my hands at the bathroom sink, I suddenly felt something in my heart say, "You know, this is the week; get ready. You'll go up for the altar call." I stopped what I was doing. It was just a thought—or maybe a whisper to my heart—but it was strong, and there was no mistaking the message.

That Sunday was the day I publicly and fully gave my heart to the Lord. It was April 15, 2006. I do not specifically recall what the pastor spoke about that morning, but without question, the Lord was speaking to me yet again, His love urging me to respond.

The tugging on my soul was so strong that it was impossible to ignore. I had no choice but to go to the altar. The pull of the Holy Spirit was like a magnet. I was surprised everyone in the building wasn't rushing to the front.

When I arrived at the altar, there was someone standing to my left. I felt like we should be holding hands. I looked to my left; it was a man. He did not look at me, and I was afraid to ask. I looked to my right, but there was no one there. I looked straight ahead. And then, in that very exact moment, I heard a sweet little voice whisper to me, "Would you mind holding my hand?" I looked again to my right, and there beside me was an adorable little old lady. She was smiling at me. I smiled back, took her hand, and said softly "I was just thinking we should all be holding hands."

What are the chances of such a sequence of events occurring? Something so beautiful could only be orchestrated by our loving God. That dear, sweet lady who wanted someone to hold her hand also fulfilled my desire to hold one. It was a demonstration of the Lord's provision for our every good desire and an example of how He never leaves or forsakes us.

"Be strong and courageous. Do not be afraid or terrified because of them, for the Lord your God goes with you; he will never leave you nor forsake you" (Deuteronomy 31:6).

The old woman's hand was more than that—it was God holding my hand. He can use anyone to touch our hearts and reassure us of His love. What a beautiful moment that altar call was for me. I gave my heart to the Lord, and He showed me once again that He was always right there and that I would never be alone.

God has spoken to me through lightning bolts and whispers, moments and miracles, even animals and songs. In fact, I believe He talks to me much more than I hear. I believe He talks to you, too, although His conversations with you may take on a different form than mine, for we each have our own journey. Regardless of His methods of communication, I urge you not to limit Him, but rather to pursue Him.

I can tell you without the slightest doubt that God is real. He loves you. He is with you always. He offers you unconditional love. It is a love greater than earthly family, stronger than the bond of a best friend, and more powerful than the fluttering of a heart in love, for He is the greatest love of all.

Freedom Found Me

by Joanna Jacob

On February 9, 2007, my life changed. In a moment, I was delivered from an addiction to alcohol that had held me captive for twenty-two years.

"When he had said this, Jesus called out in a loud voice, 'Lazarus, come out!'" (John 11:43).

Lazarus walked out of a tomb, having been dead, but he was resurrected to life by Jesus. I was a woman who, in many ways, had been dead to life due to my drinking. Jesus did for me what four treatment centers could not, and since that day, I have never been the same.

I have not written my testimony before, and in some ways, I never want to look back. But God gives each one of us a story. I believe anyone reading this who is in the grips of a secret and destructive lifestyle of addiction will find hope in total surrender to Jesus. Freedom is possible. Jesus delivers. Jesus heals. Jesus restores. His love is a force greater than any problem or mess you may think you've made of your life. He is the same yesterday, today, and forever.

Like some, my experience with drinking started at a young age. I took sips from my grandfather's beers. I was a rebellious thirteen-year-old, and it was around this time my father was diagnosed with cancer. After a five-year battle with the disease, he died. I felt alone, and consequently, sank into a dark lifestyle.

By the time I was twenty-one, I had been through treatment for drugs and alcohol three different times, including a four-month facility stay. When I turned twenty-four, I had been married, divorced, and was raising my daughter alone.

Over the next ten years, things improved. I finished school, got a good job, and was in a steady relationship. On the surface, everything appeared to be okay, but on the inside, I was empty, and things were slowly unraveling. Throughout this time, I never stopped drinking. For the most part, I got better at hiding it.

I was raised going to church. I believed in God, and I knew about Him, but He always seemed beyond my reach and far away.

In 2006, my long-term relationship ended. My daughter was suffering from health issues. I spent another week in alcohol rehab, which almost cost me my job. I had major surgery. And although it wasn't my fault, I was involved in an auto accident which totaled my vehicle. I believe this was the year God was getting my attention. I was at the bottom, broken, and simply existing. My relationship with my family was strained. I was mad at the whole world and took it out on my family as often as I could—but light was about to dawn.

I met a guy in November of 2006, and we started to date. When the subject of God came up, we decided to attend a church service together. My daughter accepted Jesus into her heart immediately. My decision to accept Christ came several weeks later. At the time, I didn't really understand what that meant, but something deep down had begun to stir. We attended church most Sundays, and slowly I found myself turning my life, and all my mess, over to Christ.

Shortly after, my soon-to-be ex-boyfriend called and said there was going to be a revival meeting, and he wanted us to be there. I initially declined, but he was adamant my daughter and I attend. I changed my mind at the last minute and decided we would go.

The evening of the revival, we got a late start and encountered major traffic delays. We arrived at the church well after the meeting started. Quietly, we found our way up the stairs and to the back of the building. I began to listen.

Before long, the preacher gave an invitation to come to Jesus, to accept Jesus, to surrender your life to Jesus. My heart screamed to God. *If you are real, help me!* In that moment, with my eyes closed, I began to see light—literally light. It was as if a layer of darkness had been peeled off of my physical body. I can't explain it, but something happened. Peace like I had never known before flooded my entire being. And I knew it was God. He was real, and He loved me. Before the night was over, my daughter and I went to the altar and received prayer. I left feeling like a new person.

I woke up the next morning, and I was different. My thoughts about alcohol and the desire to drink were gone—amazingly gone. I was able to simply stop drinking. There were no physical withdrawals like the ones I had experienced in the various rehab programs; rather, I had been delivered.

Since that day, I have continued to walk with Jesus and in this awesome miracle from God.

"But you are … a people belonging to God, that you may declare the praises of him who called you out of darkness into his wonderful light" (1 Peter 2:9).

Freedom found me.

A God-Written
Love Story

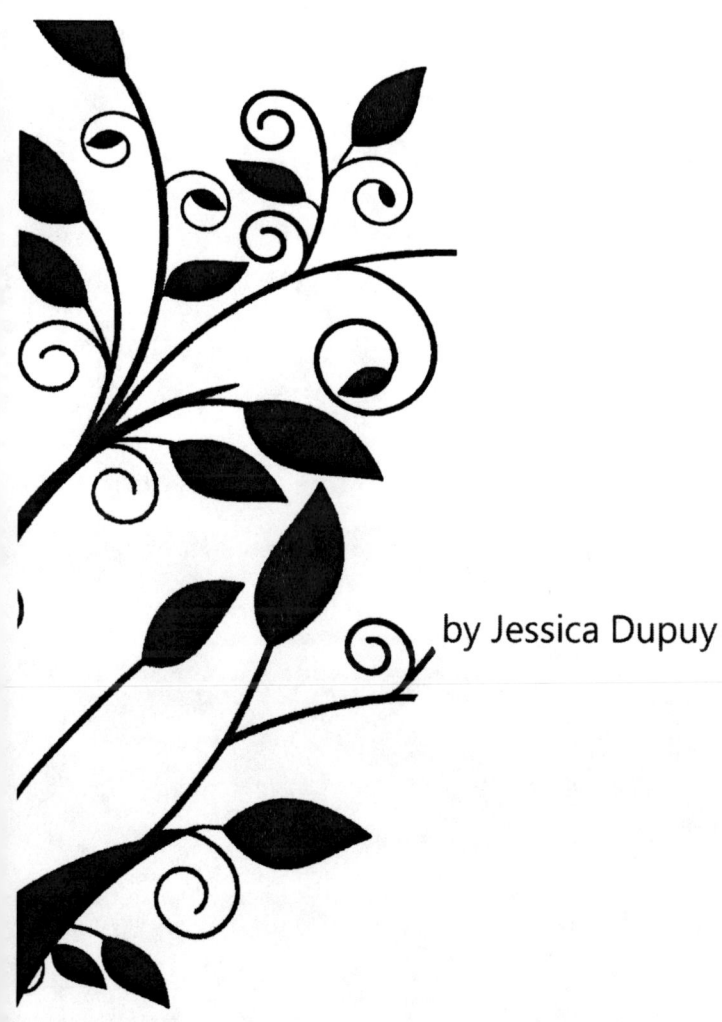

by Jessica Dupuy

D uring my teenage years, my relationship with the Lord really began to mature, and Jeremiah 29:11 spoke to my heart like no other Scripture I had ever heard.

"'For I know the plans I have for you,' declares the Lord, 'plans to prosper you and not to harm you, plans to give you a hope and a future'" (Jeremiah 29:11).

The teenage years are a time of much turmoil, excitement, and decision-making. I felt all of these things, and to know that God had my best in mind—that He had a future planned for me and that He loved me so very much—was a relief. I didn't have to figure out on my own what to do with my life; all I had to do was trust God. He would direct my path. It was then that I truly began to desire His plan for my life above all else.

I knew this meant God would also direct my dating life. As I looked around at how the world handled relationships, it was very obvious to me that there must be a better way. I knew the heartache I saw couldn't possibly be the way God intended things to be. I wanted God to write my love story, because He knew me better than anyone and would know what was best for me. I vowed not only to save my body, but also my heart for my future husband. I wanted to be able to give my future husband a heart that had been saved for him alone.

Because it was so important to me to have my parents' approval, I decided I wouldn't go forward in any relationship unless we all had a peace and certainty that the relationship would proceed to marriage. I truly believed God would show my parents the person who was right for me—even before I knew.

All my interactions with the opposite sex were kept very guarded, because I was desperate to keep my heart from getting broken by wrong relationships. During this time, I developed ideas of what kind of person I thought I needed, how the relationship would proceed, and when it would happen. I wanted to know my future mate as a friend first and be involved in ministry together. I also wanted him to have a strong relationship with God, be a man of integrity and character, love me for the person I was, and be a good listener. I thought I would end up with someone who was funny, outgoing, spontaneous, and musically talented.

I knew I was going to attend college, so I did not want to be in a relationship until after I graduated. Once, I remember telling God my plan: I would graduate, maybe work for a year or two, and then He could bring someone along. Take note of *my* plan. Even with all of my plans, I still wanted God's plan for me and knew He had my best in mind—whatever the circumstances.

Throughout the years, couples in our church would tell of how they were total opposites and had no interest in each other, but God brought them together. They said they didn't see it at first, but they were God's best for each other. I often wondered if this would end up happening to me. Would the person God had for me be completely different from what I thought I needed? I told God I would never say no to anyone He brought into my life, even if he didn't fit my idea of a mate.

During my senior year in high school, a young, very shy man named Silas started coming to our church. He was a mutual friend of some of the other youth in my church. He would always leave soon after church ended, which made it difficult to get to know him.

About a year after I first met him, we began having college and career meetings through the church. This gave the other young adults—and me—a chance to know him. It was there I first saw his deep, unwavering relationship with the Lord, his character, and his heart. We even began working in the same youth ministry together. On more than one occasion, someone pointed him out to me, saying what a great man he was and what a wonderful husband he would be. I remember thinking he would make some other woman very happy, but he wasn't my type.

I was attending college to become an elementary school teacher, still wondering what type of man God would bring along, but knowing I had a few years before I would graduate.

Little did I know that about a year and half later, God would put *me* on Silas's heart. Silas had the same convictions about dating and relationships as I did, so he began to pray. He decided he would not pursue me unless he truly had a peace from God, because he wanted to do things God's way, not his. Eight months passed, and he was still praying. I had no idea he was interested in me. By Christmas, he had a peace about talking to me but wasn't sure how to approach me. He thought he should talk to my dad first but never felt a peace about it.

One Sunday in mid-January, a group of us went out to eat after church, including Silas. I noticed he seemed particularly quiet that day. As we were leaving, he asked if he could talk to me the following Wednesday after church. I thought maybe it had something to do with the youth ministry we were involved in together. I couldn't figure out what was so important that he couldn't just call me on the phone. Deep down, I wondered what would be so significant that we had to talk in person. Did he like me? Was he going to ask me to begin a relationship?

After anxiously waiting, Wednesday finally arrived. Silas and I chatted with everyone after church until they all left. I leaned against the hood of my car, and he leaned against the church building. It was a crisp night, and my teeth chattered from the cold—but probably more from nerves. We made small talk for a while until the conversation quieted down. I looked at him, waiting for the words that could possibly alter my life forever. His hands were in his jacket pockets, and his fierce blue eyes pierced mine. He mumbled something about trying to get this out as best as possible. He then said the dreaded words. He had feelings for me—as more than a friend.

I kept a completely blank, straight face, although my insides were freaking out. All my heart's desires flashed before me. I wasn't ready for this. I wasn't even interested in Silas, but I told God I would never say no. Much to my amazement, he didn't ask to begin a relationship with me; he only asked to get to know me better as a friend and to pray about where the relationship should go from there. Somehow, that immediately took the pressure off. I told him that would be okay, which surprised even me, because I had always been very guarded in relationships with men. We exchanged phone numbers, and as we were about to leave, he handed me a gift. He said not to open it until I got home and to open the card first.

My mind was racing as I got inside the car. This wasn't just some random guy; this was a truly wonderful man who I knew already possessed all the qualities I desired in a mate. I just never considered him anything but a friend, because I thought he wasn't my type. I called my mom on the way home and asked her and my dad to wait up. I wanted to talk to them.

I climbed atop their bed and told them everything. I was panicking, although I'm not sure about what. They prayed for me, and my mom held me in her arms. The moment was a somber one. We just knew it could be real. It was scary. My parents knew Silas and truly thought that he was a man of God. They saw no problem with us talking. I decided to open the card.

The entire left side was filled with Silas's writing. He said he was writing to make sure he got his point across. He went on to say how he really wanted to get to know my family and me, and if something happened down the road, that would be great, but the most important thing to him was his relationship with the Lord and working in the ministry. He said he had been as open and honest with me as he could and only asked the same from me. He requested that if I could not see him as more than friend to please tell him. It was here I knew I had to talk to him, because I had not said anything after he expressed his feelings for me.

Somehow, everything Silas said in the card made me feel at ease. I even saw some wit I didn't know he had. I didn't feel put on the spot to start a relationship. He said he considered me "a good friend with potential." At the end, he wrote, "P.S. I gave you some food for thought, so I thought you could use a snack—a sweet snack for a sweet teacher-to-be." I opened the gift, and it was a big chocolate apple with a gummy worm. Wow! My heart melted. How thoughtful!

I called him Friday night and asked if we could meet Sunday after church. When Sunday came, I told him I thought he was a great guy and that I could have feelings for him, but I wanted God's will more than anything else. I said I wanted us to be completely honest with each other and for things to proceed slowly, since I had never even had a close friendship with a guy.

The next few weeks and months were met with many emotions. I think I experienced every emotion known to man! I even found out that God had showed him to my mom and dad at different times over the past year and a half. My main concern was twofold: discovering God's will and keeping my heart in one piece. This was one of the biggest decisions of my life. For me, beginning a relationship was like committing to marriage. I really hadn't expected this time of my life to start while I was still in college, and I worried about balancing that and a relationship. I sought God desperately for peace and an answer.

Silas and I began to talk on the phone about once a week. We also spent time with each other's families. I leaned on God's Word like never before—especially Jeremiah 29:11. Many fears arose, and there were many times I had to give them to the Lord. I struggled with this off and on. I had to trust God like never before. I wanted the answer to be clear, without doubt. I began to find myself feeling very comfortable with Silas. His family was wonderful, and he was really funny, too.

By March, Silas and I decided to meet and talk about where things stood. I was nervous, because I wasn't really sure what I was going to say. When we met, I had a peace about our relationship but still needed more time. Silas said he was ready to move forward. My heart began to feel *yes,* but I was still wanting to confirm this was God's will and not mine. I had to make sure it was what God wanted for my life and that Silas was the man God had for me.

As we approached April, I looked back over the past three months and saw I had received many confirmations about the relationship. I acted like I was waiting for God to write his name on my wall. God had shown me that this relationship had been His idea from the beginning. I had nothing to do with it. I had gotten to know this shy young man who was much more than meets the eye. I knew with all my heart that Silas would love, cherish, and take care of me. I knew I could reveal my deepest hurts and scars, and he would still love me. I saw he was what I needed even though I didn't know it at first.

I nervously called Silas on Saturday, April 30 and asked him to come over so we could talk. My parents prayed with me before I called him, and as they did, I felt the peace of God wash over me. It was as if God was saying the only reason I was in this place was because He had led me there.

As Silas and I settled in on the couch to talk, I began to ramble for a few minutes about how I had been feeling the past few months. He finally asked, "So, is that a yes?"

"Yes, it is," I said. I asked Silas to stay and have dinner with my family. He did.

When I walked Silas out to his truck that night, he asked if he could pray with me. The night was very beautiful. The wind was blowing, and the night air was cool. After he concluded the prayer, he pulled out a bouquet of roses. I was shocked. I asked him, with a laugh, what he would have done if I had said we should just be friends. He said he knew I would say yes. God had surely done a good thing.

The following summer was filled with many firsts. I managed to juggle my summer schedule so we could get to know each other better. Each day, our relationship grew, and I began to fall in love with the amazing man God had brought into my life. I saw that Silas was what I needed— even in ways I could have never imagined. By the end of the summer, the first "I love you" had been said, and we talked of engagement rings. After a storybook proposal, we got engaged on a chilly November night. I was set to graduate the following May, so we decided to get married shortly after graduation.

As I walked down the aisle on a beautiful June evening, my heart soared as I saw the man whom I had given my heart to standing there, waiting for me. His eyes were glistening, and I told God, "Thank you for doing such a great job." Yes, God surely had given me a hope and a future. That beautiful evening took place almost five years ago. Every day, I'm grateful that I followed God's plan and not mine. I truly feel Silas and I were a match made in heaven.

My challenge to you is this: Have you surrendered your life to Christ? If you have, have you surrendered every aspect of your life: your finances, your goals, and your future? I promise you won't be disappointed if you follow God's plan. Even if you've followed your own way up until now, it's not too late. God will honor your submission to Him and His will. Does that mean your life will be perfect and free from conflict? Of course it doesn't. Silas and I know we are not perfect people; we are just perfect for each other.

My hope and desire is that you first seek Christ. Then allow Him to bring your very own "Prince Charming" to you. I can testify that God's will for your life is better than any storybook romance that has ever been imagined. Allow God to write your love story.

"And so we know and rely on the love God has for us. God is love. Whoever lives in love lives in God, and God in him" (1 John 4:16).

Once I Was Lost, but Now I Am Found

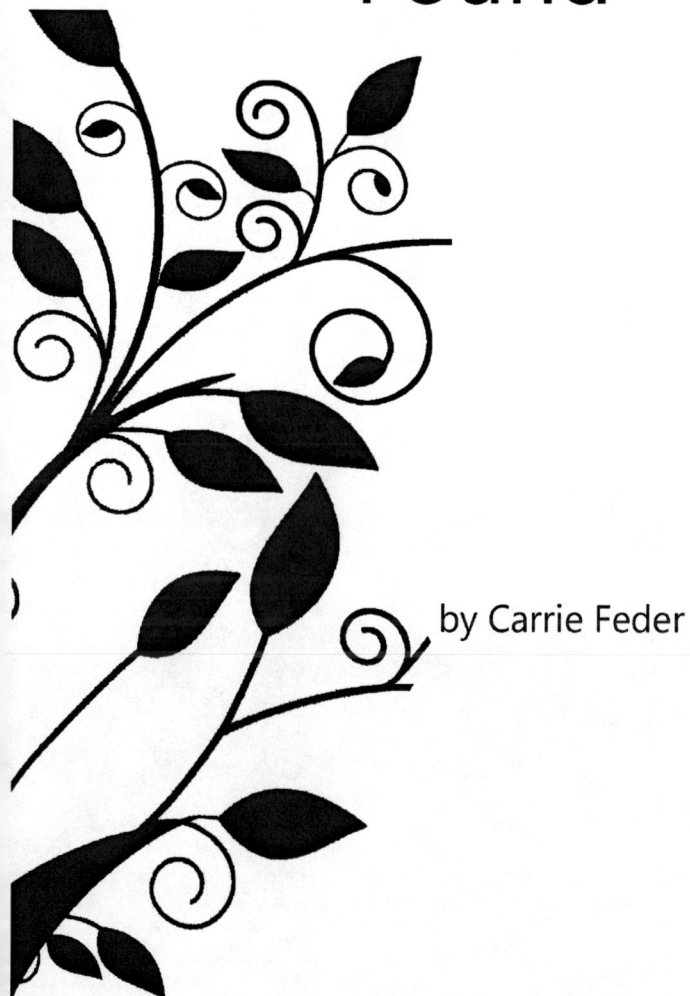

by Carrie Feder

I have a story that I would like to share with you. It is a story that will challenge you to see the love of God and how He has moved in my life.

My name is Carrie Feder. I'm in my thirties and have recently gotten married. Words can't describe how thankful I am to be alive and married to such a faithful and wonderful husband like my Matthew.

If it wasn't for the kindness and goodness of God, I wouldn't be telling you about my life today. *"But when the kindness and love of God our Savior appeared, he saved us, not because of righteous things we had done, but because of his mercy. He saved us through the washing of rebirth and renewal by the Holy Spirit"* (Titus 3:4–5).

When I share my testimony, I usually get two reactions. One reaction is an overwhelming sense of the love of God and excitement about how He revealed His saving power to me, a sinner. The other reaction is one that saddens me, because my testimony is questioned, judged, and challenged by religious or traditional views and can cause the person to miss the whole point, which is to see God's mighty, saving power and love.

I share my testimony boldly and without shame, because I have to tell people about His love and forgiveness. I am not the same person anymore. My old lifestyle has passed away, and I am a new creation in Christ. *"Therefore, if anyone is in Christ, he is a new creation; the old has gone, and the new has come!"* (2 Corinthians 5:17)

I no longer feel the weight of guilt and shame that use to cast its shadow on me. Instead, I feel as though the person of the past I'm telling you about is not me, but someone else. God has restored me. He has done much in my life, and I have to share my story with others.

I have to admit that I too am challenged not to judge people because of where they have been, where they are, or what they are walking through. Rather, I try to understand their stories—their own personal journeys of life. After what God has saved me from, I would be a hypocrite to not listen and try to understand the road others have traveled.

I must begin my story by explaining that God allowed me to go through seven years of living in my own personal torment and pain. I was living my life the way I wanted and was self-destructing. At fourteen years old, I began to experience the pressures of growing up. I began to rebel against my parents and God and do the things I wanted to do. I began to experiment with sex, drinking, and eventually, drugs. I started smoking weed when I was fifteen. All through high school, I was very athletic and played sports, but during the off-seasons, I would hang out with the wrong crowd and feel tempted to do the activities of those I was around.

At fourteen, I stopped going to church. My parents gave my sister and me the choice. We could decide whether we wanted to continue to go or not. They were tired of us complaining and whining about going. So naturally, when we were given the choice, we said we didn't want to go. Church was boring. I fell asleep. The Word of God wasn't exactly preached, so I didn't see the point. During the service, a Scripture would be read, but that was it. I didn't feel God. I didn't sense His presence. I would go and serve my hour, thinking I was doing Him a favor.

The only thing I liked about church was going out to eat afterwards. In fact, the only time I would feel a warm cozy feeling was at the end of service, when we would sing the last song. I remember wanting to experience God's presence as a child. I would stare at the gold cross in the middle of the sanctuary and beg God to reveal Himself to me. I wanted to feel Him. I wanted to experience His love and presence. I would feel a little something like peace, and then it was over. In total, I might have had five minutes of peace and one tear expressing my gratitude to Him. At the time, I couldn't explain it, but I desired more. I knew there must be more to Him—more than reciting the same prayers and singing the same hymns.

I knew Jesus had been resurrected, but I didn't understand why. I heard about it, but I couldn't relate to it. I was confused. I had heard of the Holy Spirit, too, but only in repetitious prayers we said every week in church. He wasn't talked about; He wasn't explained. We only heard His name. Sometimes, growing up, He sort of scared me. I would ask myself, *Who is the Holy Spirit? Is He a ghost in the corner of the church? What does He have to do with anything?* Jesus was a man and God, and God was God, but the Holy Spirit confused me. What I didn't understand, I left alone. I simply forgot about Him, because He wasn't really mentioned.

I grew up in church, but I didn't have my own knowledge of God. I only knew what I was told. I didn't have a personal relationship with Him. I knew He was important. I knew He existed, but I didn't understand what He had to do with me. How was He relevant in my life? I would pray to Him when I was in trouble and plead for Him to get me out of a mess, but that was it.

It's not that I didn't want a relationship with God. I just didn't know how to have one. I saw Him as the big God who made the world—the sky, the stars, and the ocean. I thought He was busy with the earth and all the other people on it. I was not important. I believed the lie that I was not significant to Him. It was a lie. I had no idea Psalm 139 explained in full detail just how important each person is to the Lord.

As I grew older, I began to question God's very existence. I saw pain and suffering in my life and in the lives of those around me, and I couldn't understand why God would allow it. I had an unrealistic expectation that nothing bad would ever happen to me if God loved me. I was wrong to think I could be invisible to pain and suffering.

At the age of eighteen, I became enthralled by a life of drugs, drinking, and sex. Where these things were once experimental, they turned into ways of escape from the pressures and problems of life. I got addicted to ecstasy on the spring break trip of my senior year in 1998. I was instantly hooked. On this drug, you feel euphoria and love for everyone. You feel accepted. Ironically, that was really all I wanted—to feel loved and accepted and have the freedom to be myself. It's not that I didn't have people around that loved me. I did. I had wonderful parents, who cared for and loved me, but I chose to escape to a fantasy world of love and acceptance, and all I needed to get there was a little pill.

I remember a couple of times when my mom asked me if I was on anything—any kind of drug. Being the great actress that I am, I would lie, looking right into her eyes and act shocked she would ask such a thing. I manipulated her and made her feel bad for asking. I was deceptive to both my parents and constantly put on a facade that everything was fine. I told them lie after lie.

Once I got addicted to ecstasy, nothing else mattered. Life outside of the drug didn't matter. I became numb. I tried to find happiness in sex, drugs, and guys. I questioned God's existence. I pondered Him being in heaven while I was on earth. I had never truly read the Bible on my own, and I didn't understand God. I felt abandoned by Him. I felt He didn't care about me. He had too many people on earth to worry about, and my little life didn't mean much. These are the things you think when you don't know Him.

I was trying to find my way. I was trying to experience freedom outside of my parents' leadership and direction. I was a strong-willed child and was ready to find my own identity and life. During that summer—the summer of my senior year—I was consumed with drinking, drugs, and sex to the point that all the morals I had completely left. After numerous sexual partners and indulging my lusts, I became pregnant.

I was going to start college in the fall and wanted to pursue my dream of becoming a veterinarian. I was a child in many ways, and the thought of becoming a mother was terrifying. I saw all of my dreams and aspirations going up in smoke.

My thoughts raced. The baby would only cause more pain and sorrow. I couldn't let a baby ruin my life. I mixed and used so many drugs in my body that I reasoned I had probably already destroyed it in my womb. The father of the child—the guy I thought was the father—seemed to always be drunk. So how could we raise a child together when I had only known him for a month or so? And at that point, the baby was only a few inches long, so was an abortion really killing a child? If I did it quickly, then I could erase the situation. I could forget it ever happened, and no one would know. I would cover it up and keep living my life. All these thoughts went through my head, and were my way of justifying what I was about to do. Abortion was the only option in my mind. I thought it was the only way I could live my life and keep pursuing my dreams.

I will never forget walking into the clinic on September 3, 1998. The place was so dark that it was as if I could literally see darkness and evil. The moment I walked in, all I wanted to do was leave. Instead, I stayed and anxiously looked around the clinic, wondering if I really wanted to go through with it.

As I waited, I heard the receptionist ask a woman, "So, this is your third abortion?" A part of me was surprised it wasn't her first time, but another part of me thought, *Well, if she has had three, how bad could it be? If it is so bad, why is she back again?*

I walked back to the examining room. Alone for a moment, I changed into a patient gown. The nurse walked in and injected a fluid into my arm. The next thing I knew, I was waking up, asking if it was over. The nurse was cold and impersonal. Everything about the experience was cold and dark. As I left the clinic, I saw protesters. They had huge signs and were yelling, "God loves you!" I was out of it. Still heavily medicated, I had a hard time reading their signs.

I got into the car, and a lady came running up to my window. She looked at me with compassion and love in her eyes. "God loves you! He loves you!" she screamed. I just looked at her with a blank stare. I asked myself, *How does He love me? Why does He love me? Do you know what I just did? How does He love me after what I just did? There's no way He loves me now.*

I don't recall what the woman looked like, what she was wearing, or any detail of her face; I only remember how she looked at me with such love and compassion as she said to me, "God loves you!"

There were moments like that where I can now recognize God. He was trying to reach out to me. He was trying to get His children to help me. He was trying to talk to me by putting them in my path. He was using real Christians—ones who lived for Him.

After the abortion, I sank very deeply into depression. I had a lot of shame and guilt. I couldn't bear to look at myself. Every time I looked into a mirror, all I saw was shame and guilt. All I saw was a murderer. I didn't recognize myself. I was gone. I just existed in a life of pain. The sweet, happy, innocent child I used to be was gone. I was lost. There were many times I would think to myself, *Who am I? Who have I become? What have I become?* My questions were answered in my head with more lies.

I had thought of the abortion as a quick solution to the problem, but the abortion made everything worse. I began to feel the weight of my shame, guilt, and sin. I couldn't escape the overwhelming reality of all the wrong decisions I had made. I started using more drugs, hoping they would numb my pain. Life was getting too hard. It was overwhelming, and I had to find an escape.

One night, I was hanging out with some friends. As we were driving to the club, we were talking about getting high and how much fun we were going to have. While we were on the interstate, I looked up and saw a huge billboard on the side of the road. I stared at it with conviction. It read, "Is the road you are on leading to heaven or hell?"

There was something about that billboard that shook my entire being. In fact, I scoffed at it, because for a moment, I questioned if I should be going to the club and doing drugs.

I believed everyone who died would go to heaven, because God was a forgiving God. He might let me suffer in the afterlife a little, but eventually, I'd get there. I didn't believe in Satan or demons. I only believed in God and angels. I believed what I wanted, and I only wanted to believe the good. I didn't hear a lot about Satan except that he was the figure in cartoons with a red suit and pitchfork. He wasn't real, and if he wasn't real, hell wasn't real. How could a good, loving God send someone to hell? That wasn't God. He wasn't mean. He was the God who made all the beautiful things like the sky, stars, and trees. How could this God send someone to hell? No, that's where I was—in torment, pain, and suffering. Hell on earth is what existed in my mind. I didn't believe God would allow anyone to be tormented for eternity.

From eighteen to twenty years of age, I was wrapped around drugs, alcohol, and sex. My life was a continuous cycle of clubs, parties, and immoral behavior. I was in a lot of emotional pain. Tormented with the replay of the clinic, I felt burdened with guilt and shame. I got to the point where I couldn't deal with it anymore. I was hopeless and confused. I was lost in my own prison of unbearable shame and suffering.

As far as my beliefs, I was confused. I didn't really know what I believed, and because of this, I would adopt other beliefs. I would unknowingly take pieces from other religions and incorporate those beliefs into my own. This confusion caused me to believe that all paths led to God and heaven. I began to believe that if I died, God would give me a chance to redeem myself. He would understand what I was going through and accept me. I believed I could be reincarnated, come back as someone else, and live a better life. I believed if you committed suicide, you would go to purgatory—not hell—and wait until God said it was okay to go to heaven. I began to believe that there really wasn't a punishment for taking my own life. I began to ponder these things. All of the pain and suffering I caused myself led me to ask questions. I began to think, *God, do you really exist? Are you really there?*

Each time September 3 came around I was reminded of what I had done. I dreaded that time of year, because it brought back every emotion, memory, and argument the enemy had spoken to me.

In July of 2000, at the age of twenty, I got really sick. I was having a hard time sleeping at night because I was sick and because I had been without peace for so long. The sickness made me unable to sleep for an entire week. I was up constantly through the night, and with only a few hours of sleep for the week, I felt I was losing my mind.

Once my sleeping patterns were messed up, I became fearful of the night—especially of the time to go to bed. I was afraid I wouldn't sleep. I became delirious. By the end of the week, I was thinking irrational thoughts and contemplating the act of suicide.

That Friday, my parents were going out of town. I knew my boyfriend and I would be alone. We would have the house to ourselves for the entire weekend. On Friday morning, as my parents said goodbye, I was determined to end my life that night. I didn't know how I was going to do it, but I was going to take my life into my own hands and end it. I almost succeeded.

Around midnight, when I thought my boyfriend was asleep; I got up and began to search the house for a method. I went into my parents' bedroom. Inside their walk-in closet, I saw my dad's pistol. I picked up the pistol and moved my fingers over it. I had it aimed at my mouth, and suddenly I had a thought—an impression. *Don't do this. Don't do this. They have been so good to you. They are the best parents; don't do it. They don't deserve this.*

I put the pistol back and left the room. I headed toward the kitchen and grabbed the biggest bottle of pills I could find. It was a five hundred-count bottle of aspirin. I thought to myself, *This is it. I will do it like this.* I began to take handfuls of aspirin, one after the other. Pills fell everywhere around me. I continued to take them—four or five at a time. By the time I finished, almost half of the bottle was gone. I scrambled to pick up the fallen aspirins. My boyfriend could hear me in the kitchen and asked what I was doing. I didn't answer. I went back to my room and lay down on the bed. I told him, "I just took some medicine; I'm fine. Everything is fine. Let's just go to sleep. Everything will be better tomorrow."

He persisted. He said, "Carrie, what's going on? What's wrong?" I tried to find an excuse so he would leave me alone. I began to explain that I was tired and needed to sleep, but my speech was slurred. I could barely talk at that point. It was difficult to breathe. My boyfriend turned on the light and would not leave me alone. His persistence saved my life.

Finally, I confessed what I had done. My boyfriend grabbed me and rushed me to the hospital half a mile away. We burst into the emergency section of the hospital, and the doctors took me back immediately. They had to carry me, because I couldn't stand. I was too weak. They asked my name, and all I could say was, "Carrie."

The doctors brought me into a room with small windows all around. They immediately gave me a charcoal-like substance. They tried to get me to throw up, but I was too weak to try. As they talked to me, I began to close my eyes. They pleaded with me to stay awake, but I was too sleepy. I was ready to die. I closed my eyes and saw white—only white. I began to feel different. The pain was gone. Finally, the pain was gone. I was able to escape the pain.

In the middle of this feeling, I suddenly woke up to something being jammed down my throat. I felt like I was choking to death. I looked around to find several doctors and nurses around me. I was lost, confused, and didn't know where I was. I began to choke. I was very frightened. I began to fight the emergency staff as they tried to get a huge tube down my throat. There was a nurse to my left. She spoke to me firmly but was comforting at the same time. "Carrie, if you don't let this tube go down, you will die from choking." I tried to relax and trust them. The tube entered my stomach, and they pumped out the aspirin.

Once the procedure was complete, they wheeled my bed to an isolated room, where they kept me in observation for twenty-four hours. During that time, I had several people come in and talk with me. They tried to find out who I was, and they wanted to know why I would take such a drastic measure to try to end my life.

I was careful not to say much. I wanted to figure out if they knew I had been taking drugs. I was scared. I didn't know if they had tested me and found out I was an ecstasy user.

When they realized I wasn't going to talk to a doctor, they brought in a social worker. She was very nice and understanding. She asked me questions in a non-invasive way. After several minutes of dialogue, I asked if she could keep a question confidential. She agreed. I asked if they had found ecstasy in my blood samples. She said no but wanted to know why I was curious. I explained that I was not an addict but just an occasional user. She inquired how often I used, and I told her not as much as I used to—only once or twice a month.

When she left my room, I remember feeling a peace that surpassed all understanding. I looked up at my IV bag and thought, *How ironic—in my darkest hour, I feel the most at peace.* It baffled me that in the moment when I felt most abandoned by God, I somehow felt His peace. It didn't make any sense!

A doctor walked into my room. He told me he was admitting me into a rehab hospital and wanted me to sign the documentation. I asked if I had to go, and he said, "If you don't admit yourself, I will. You are a danger to yourself, and you need help." I denied it. I told him I wanted to go home. He said, "Carrie, this is the best thing for you." I shamefully signed the paperwork and asked if I could call my parents.

The conversation I had with my parents was very difficult. I could barely contain myself as I tried to explain what was going on. I remember my dad being in complete shock and my mom crying in the background. They were devastated. I told them that I wasn't sure where I was going, but I would contact them as soon as I could. I would get my boyfriend to tell them where I was being taken. My parents were three states away on business. I was concerned they would have a hard time driving the long hours home after hearing such horrible news.

As the hospital prepared to transfer me, I was finally able to rest. The night had been long, and I was delirious from no sleep earlier in the week as well. Unbeknownst to me, however, I had a visitor in my room. It was a male nurse. He leaned up against the wall and had a noticeable look on his face. It was a look I won't ever forget. It was a look of astonishment—of surprise. I'm not sure what he was thinking, but I awoke to him staring at me. Maybe he was looking at the clothes I was wearing and thinking, *This girl is athletic; she has a volleyball t-shirt on with her name and team number on the back. She was on her high school's volleyball team. Why is she here? What could be going on in her life that she feels she has to end it?* I have no idea what he was thinking, but looking at his face of disbelief, I could tell he didn't understand.

I had problems. I had issues. The nurse didn't know what I had gone through. He didn't know that I had an abortion. He didn't know how much torment was in my life. He didn't know me at all. How could he lean against the wall and pass judgment on me?

I gave him a harsh look. When he saw my expression, he fidgeted and left. To this day, I don't know who he was. I don't remember seeing him before or after that moment. Was he passing judgment, or was he led by God to pray for me? I may never know until I get to heaven. Regardless, he struck a chord in me. He affected me, and I remember him to this day. I don't think we realize how much we truly affect others.

During my transport process, one of the guys who worked in the EMS truck was a good friend of mine from high school. He didn't believe I was being taken to an inpatient rehab hospital for having tried to commit suicide. The minute I saw him, I covered my face, because I felt so much shame. He saw my embarrassment and assured me he would keep it confidential.

God placed my friend there when I needed him. He drove around the city and waited until the hospital was able to deliver me to a decent unit. He refused to take me to the place they initially wanted. He said, "No, she is not going there. I will drive around this city all day until a better place opens up. She needs to go to a better place than that." I felt very thankful he was there. He brought me comfort in the midst of my tragedy.

The first night was the hardest. The staff led me to a room where I was able to be alone. They gave me towels, a blanket, and a pillow. They told me I could lie down. It was obvious I was exhausted, but when I walked into my room, all I could do was cry. I looked around and saw a window. I could see trees and grass; they comforted me for a moment. I looked out the window and cried aloud, challenging God. "God, if you even exist, help me! Help me!"

I had never felt so alone. I had never felt so abandoned. I truly was at rock bottom. My parents couldn't get me out of this mess. There was no one who could get me out of this kind of trouble. I was finally stuck with the consequences. I was in so much despair that it was hard to breathe my next breath. I lay down on the bed and cried. I cried for what felt like hours until finally, I slept.

I woke up to a nurse inviting me to dinner at the center of the unit. I asked if I could talk to my parents or see my boyfriend. She said my parents were on their way, and my boyfriend was at my house, getting my clothes and toiletries. She informed me of the hospital policies: I could have visitors from 6:00–7:00 p.m., and I could use the phone for ten minutes each day. I told her I wasn't hungry and wanted to stay in my room. She said she understood and left.

During my stay, I was put on several antidepressants. In total, I was given four pills and one sleeping tablet. I was so medicated that often I had a hard time comprehending conversations. My mom could tell I was becoming disoriented. She knew I was not myself. One time, she asked me what month it was, and I told her it was May. She looked at me and said, "Baby, it's July."

During one specific visit with my parents, my mom handed me a green Gideon's Bible. She said, "Baby, this is all I can give you right now. I feel we have given you everything we could—a good childhood, a good home, a good family—but maybe we didn't give you more of what you needed the most, religion and God."

I looked at her and my dad and told them how much I loved them. I told them that they were great parents and how sorry I was to have caused this much pain in their lives. I could see the sorrow on their faces. They looked like they were barely keeping it together. At that moment, I felt like I had ultimately failed them as their baby. I felt deep regret for making them go through such sorrow. I longed for the days when they were proud of me and the joy that I had once brought them. At that moment, all I could see was their pain. All I could see was hurt in their eyes. I felt like a failure as a daughter. I told my mom I would take the Bible and read it. I accepted it with open arms.

Several times at group lunch or dinner, I felt alone, even while I sat amongst all the other patients. I would open my Bible and try to read. One time, I opened up the book and fell on a page about sacrificing lambs and goats. I thought to myself, *That's gross. Why is that in here, and how does that relate to me?* It was a part in the Bible that talked about how the priests of the Old Testament used to give their sacrifices to God. I didn't keep reading. I didn't understand the meaning. I looked further and found the book of Psalms. These verses seemed a lot easier to understand. I read, and as I began to read, there were certain words that really hit home. David was crying out to God about his despair and his sorrows, and I thought, *I can relate to this guy. That's how I feel right now.*

I became hungry for God. I began to search for answers about Him. When a priest, nun, or pastor would come into the rehab unit, I would migrate toward them. They attracted me. They had smiles on their faces. They had peace. I didn't know at the time what it was exactly, but it compelled me. I was drawn to them. Now I know it was Jesus. It was the love of God. They would come and offer prayers or counsel. All you had to do was ask, so I began to ask for both.

I remember having a conversation with a pastor one time. He asked me about my relationship with God. I said, "Well, He's up there, and I'm down here." He asked me to explain what I meant, and all I could say was, "Well, that's it." He proceeded to tell me that God loves me and that He is with me. I thought, *Mister, you don't know about me. You don't know what I've done. God isn't with me. He has left me. He has forgotten me. Nope, God doesn't really love me. Not me, maybe everyone else, but not me.*

I was harsh to his words and counsel. I was bitter. I was mad at God. I wasn't taking responsibility for my actions, but instead I was blaming God for all the wrong choices I had made. I listened to the pastor, and he prayed for me. I remember crying during his prayer, as little by little, I began to have hope. The hard ground of my heart was beginning to soften towards God.

One day during our inpatient arts program, something special happened. We were allowed to have arts and crafts time to get our minds off of our problems and to help express ourselves in a healthy and fun environment. I was excited about this, because I had always wanted to paint!

I was told to pick any ceramic piece I wanted, and I was very careful in my selection. I wanted one I would remember and cherish. I probably took longer than anyone else in selecting a piece. I chose a little angel boy holding a lamb. There was something special about this piece. It brought me comfort. The little boy looked peaceful, and the lamb was very gentle in his arms. I decided to paint that one.

At the time, I didn't know Jesus was referred to as the Lamb of God. I learned this a few years down the road. In fact, the first time I heard Jesus referred to as the Lamb of God, I instantly remembered the ceramic figurine I had painted in the hospital. It reassured me that Jesus was with me the whole time.

As I was painting, the counselor came up to me and smiled. She said, "You are such a gentle and caring person."

I looked at her in amazement and asked, "What?" She told me again, she thought I was kind and gentle. I thought to myself, *Lady, you just don't know me.* But instead, I asked her why she said that.

She replied, "Look at the one you chose. You could have picked anything in the room, yet you chose the little angel boy holding a lamb."

I didn't think much of it and said, "It brings me comfort."

She smiled and said, "You are a gentle person."

I don't regret being in the rehab hospital. I don't regret it at all. There were times when God showed me He was right there, even though I didn't know it.

Another example of God's existence happened when I was reading my green Gideon's Bible. One of the patients came and sat with me. We had just finished our meal and had a few minutes to sit and be still. So I read. As I read, he put his hand on my arm and said, "Carrie, you are the only one in here with any hope. Don't lose that. You have hope."

I looked at him and said, "What do you mean, I have hope? No, I do not."

He said, "Yes you do. Look at you; you are reading this. This is the Bible—the Word of God. And you are reading it. Read it aloud, Carrie."

I asked, "Really? You really want me to?"

The other patients sitting around the table chimed in and said, "Oh yes, please read it to us." So I began to read aloud. I read, and they all listened to the Psalm. As I read, tears began to flow from the eyes of one of the patients. Seeing how it touched her, I kept reading. Everyone listened intently. They were desperate to hear what the Bible said, and although I didn't really understand it, I knew we all needed to hear it.

After I was done reading, the patient who asked me to read looked at me and said, "Carrie, you do have hope. You do. Jesus is with you." As he was talking, he said, "You won't believe this!"

"What?" I asked.

"Carrie, there is a cross on your nose! A cross, Carrie!" I thought to myself, *Man, just when I think I'm talking to someone who is sane, he starts acting crazy. This guy is crazy.* He persisted. He asked, "You don't believe me?"

I said, "I'm sorry; I don't."

He wouldn't stop. "Okay, go look in the mirror in your bathroom—look at your nose!"

To appease him, I went. Little did I know that he was right—there was a cross on my nose! I looked up and down my face, moved my face in every possible angle, and thought, *How did this get here? Where did this come from? What is a cross doing on my nose?* I ran back and told him, "I don't know how this got here! I didn't have a cross on my nose a few days ago! I didn't have this on my nose Friday morning! How did this get here? Where did this come from?"

I began to ask questions. I knew I had freckles, but I'd never had them in the shape of a cross. And I looked in the mirror a lot, so if someone would have known, it would have been me. This question was one that stayed unanswered until a few years later.

I could feel the oppression in the hospital. I didn't understand how I could feel it, but I could. I could feel evil, and I could feel good. This was particularly interesting, because I didn't believe in demons, and I didn't think you could hear God's voice. I simply didn't believe in those things.

One night, while in the hospital, I walked towards the TV area when I heard someone call my name. "Carrie." I heard it loud and clear.

I asked, "What?" I looked around, but there was no one there. I didn't hear it again that night. That voice didn't make me fearful, but there was another time a voice I heard did. There were times I felt I was losing my mind. I was hearing voices.

When I got out of the hospital, everything looked much brighter. The trees were so tall! The grass was so green! The sky was so beautiful! I used to take all of these things for granted. But once I left, I felt different. I began to think, *Okay, some things are going to change. I'm not going to drink anymore, and no more drugs. I am going to find a church, and I am going to go.* I told my boyfriend that if he wanted to be in my life, we wouldn't be going to parties or clubs, drinking, or doing drugs. He agreed.

A couple of months later, I started to feel tormented again. I had a hard time sleeping, and sleeping pills weren't working. I felt the most tormented at night. During the day, I kept myself busy, but the night was a different story. At night, I had to confront all of my burdens. Sometimes I left the TV on to drown out my own issues or listened to music—whatever kept my mind on something else. I was very heavily burdened. No pill was going to keep that heavy feeling away.

Eventually it caught up to me. One night, I cried out to my mom. I couldn't sleep, and when I did sleep, I had terrible dreams. Mom came to me and said, "Carrie, I see a pastor on TV during the news. I think you should go talk to him. Maybe he can help you."

I told her, "Okay, I will. I need to talk to someone; maybe he can help. I feel like I'm losing my mind."

The next day, I called the church of this certain pastor. A receptionist answered. She said the pastor wasn't available to take my call, but she could have an associate pastor call me back. I said that would be okay. When the phone call came, I wasn't home. For a few days, we kept missing each other. Finally, Mom gave him my work number and told him to call me there.

When I got the phone call at work, he introduced himself. I was surrounded by other people in the office and was uncomfortable. I spoke quietly as I explained I was having problems and needed to talk to someone. He offered to meet with me in person, but I was reluctant. He sounded like a sincere man. He sounded compassionate, understanding, and kind, but I was too embarrassed to meet with anyone in person. He could tell I wasn't open to the idea, so instead he asked if he could pray for me. I said yes. I was relieved to receive prayer. I needed a lot of that.

As he began to pray, I began to weep. I was still surrounded by other people in the office and was afraid they would think I wasn't acting professional. I kept thinking, *This is not the time to have an emotional breakdown.* It was not an appropriate environment to cry on the telephone. I was at work and tried with every fiber of my being to stay in control and not weep uncontrollably.

But God used this man to speak to me. God used the words of this pastor to show me that He understood and that He loved me. I could feel mercy—God's abundant mercy and grace.

In the few minutes we spoke, I knew this pastor was a compassionate man. I knew he was sincere and genuinely cared about my well-being. As we ended the conversation, he invited me to church. I told him I would go.

Later that evening, I told my boyfriend, "I want to go to church this weekend. I found one, and I'd like to go visit." I could tell he wasn't thrilled, but he agreed to go.

On Saturday night, I said to my boyfriend, "Okay, we are going to church tomorrow." He was spending the night, so he said that would be okay. When morning came, he tried to keep us from going. He used excuses to justify why we needed to sleep in. But I was persistent and said, "No, I'm going. Stay here if you want, but I'm going." He got up and got dressed. He wasn't in a hurry to get there on time, which bothered me. I didn't like to be late anywhere, much less church. I felt it was disrespectful, so naturally, I was upset that we were running late.

As we walked into the church on February 4, 2001, I was amazed! Through the double doors, I saw a concert going on! Well, it was like a concert. I saw a band, a singer, drums, and guitars. I thought to myself, *What is this? What is this music? This is awesome!*

I began to get chills all over my body, and my eyes were huge with excitement and disbelief. I couldn't believe a church could be so cool— it was like a rock concert for Jesus! There were many people, and they were actually worshipping! They weren't just sitting there; they were participating. They were engaged with the music, and they were worshipping God!

Then I felt angry. Anger in church—yes, I was angry. I was angry I had never experienced this before—that I had been completely oblivious to this kind of church. I was accustomed to four-hundred-year-old hymns sung in soprano. I'm not trying to make fun of the hymns, because there are many really good ones, but this band had sopranos, altos, tenors, and bass singers. It was a song I could actually sing. And you could even see the words on the screens. The songs were full of life, joy, and excitement! They were full of passion. They spoke to me. These were songs I could relate to. These were my first reactions as I walked inside the sanctuary. My second reaction was, *Finally, I am home.*

I will never forget one song in particular that spoke volumes to me. It was a song that I believe God used to speak directly to me. It broke me. As I listened to the music and read the words displayed on the screen, I began to cry. I began to weep. It was like I couldn't hold it in any longer. I had to let it go. I couldn't contain myself anymore. I had to release the emotions! I had to release the tears.

The words ministered to me in a deep, healing way. I felt like God took His hand, placed it on me, and began to heal me immediately. For the first time, I realized, *God, you do understand. This is how I feel!*

The words of the song described a person who was having a conversation with God. In the conversation, the person describes how he is struggling to figure out what life is for. He has a hard time staying in control and holds back tears, trying to keep it together. Then there was a part of the song where God asked this person if he would worship and bow before the Lord and King. God asked him if he would love God and give Him his heart.

When I heard these words, I couldn't help but let go. I was tired of my way. I was tired of self-destructing. I needed Jesus. I needed God. I needed salvation. I needed to be saved from this life of sin and shame. I wanted to be rid of the burden of my sins. I wanted peace. I wanted to be happy again. I wanted to be free. I was done living my way, and at that moment, I knew I had to surrender to Jesus. I knew I had to give Him my life. For the first time, I realized why Jesus died on the cross! This was the first time I heard the gospel preached in such an understanding way. For the first time, I realized I was a sinner in need of a savior.

During the service, the pastor spoke about why Jesus died on the cross. He died for me. He died for my sins. He died for the sins of the world. Because God loved the world so much, He sent His only Son to die on the cross in my place. He took my sin and shame and shed His blood for me, and if I accepted Him into my life and into my heart, His blood would wash away all of my sin and shame. And He would give me a new life—a life in Him.

For the first time, my eyes were opened. For the first time, I understood what the cross meant to me and for my life. I had never heard it stated so simply. I had never realized that it was for me—He died and rose again.

After hearing the message and listening to those words, I decided that I had never accepted Jesus into my life. I was given an opportunity to ask Him into my heart and life. I was faced with a decision—to boldly walk down the aisle and confess that I needed Jesus or remain in the seat next to my boyfriend.

As the pastor made the invitation to go to the front to accept Jesus, I heard a voice that said, "Go! Don't look back; just go!" It wasn't forceful or loud but full of excitement and passion. It was a quickening that got me up and moving. I was scared that I might not have another opportunity like that again, so I quickly walked to the front through the blur of tears that wouldn't stop pouring out of my eyes.

I gave my heart to the Lord that day. On February 4, 2001, my name was written in the Lamb's Book of Life. I knew from that day forward, I was changed.

God began to do a good work in me immediately. One week after I was saved, I was water baptized. The pastor doing the baptisms that night was none other than the associate pastor who invited me to the church! I couldn't believe it. I couldn't believe he was going to baptize me. Had he not been so caring and compassionate on the phone, I never would have given my heart to the Lord that weekend—and there he was, a week later, baptizing me. I was floored. This was not a coincidence. I was amazed how God used this pastor in my life, and I was thankful he was going to be the one to baptize me.

A week after my water baptism, I was filled with the Holy Spirit at church. I didn't know you could have the Holy Spirit live and exist inside of you. That was new to me. When I heard this, I said, "Well, I want that!" I didn't understand what it meant, but my Bible study leader showed me Scriptures and helped me understand what it meant to be filled with the Holy Spirit.

There were many people God put in my path. Although I simply can't mention them all, I do remember them and all they did for me. I will always be grateful. I know one day, I will be spending eternity with them, rejoicing.

About a month or so after I was saved, I went on a women's encounter retreat with the church. It blew my mind. There were many messages and songs that spoke to me. Every time I entered into worship, I cried. I felt God's love and comfort surrounding me. It was like a warm blanket. I felt safe and secure. The desire I longed for as a child—to feel His presence—was a reality for me.

As the weekend progressed, I learned I could no longer continue living a life of sexual sin. Sex before marriage was not right, and God detested it. I always knew before I got saved that it wasn't right, but I didn't think I'd go to hell because of it. That now concerned me.

My relationship with my boyfriend concerned me. It seemed he didn't want anything to do with God or church. He even fussed at me that Sunday for giving my heart to the Lord. He told me I was being too dramatic and should have stayed in my seat. He was upset with me for that. I think he was scared of losing me to God.

The whole time I was on the encounter retreat, I got a reoccurring message: I needed to break up with my boyfriend. I made excuses to myself. *He's been with me through all my drama and pain. He's a good guy. He's caring, affectionate, and stable. No, I need him around. He can stay.* But the message continued. I tried to get around the fact, but I knew in my heart that the relationship needed to end. He and I were going two separate directions. He didn't want God, and I wanted God with all of my heart. I even had a woman lean over to me at the retreat and say, "God is telling you something, isn't He?" I thought, *What? How does she know He is telling me something?* Occurrences like this made me realize being a Christian is cool. It's an adventure!

When I got home from the retreat, I tried to break up with my boyfriend. He was devastated. He cried and pleaded for me to let him stick around. Feeling sad and not wanting to hurt him, I said, "Okay."

But as time passed it started to become clear to me that I couldn't have God and my boyfriend. It wasn't going to work. God wanted all of my life—even that relationship. The decision was hard. It was very hard.

One night, while we were hanging out together in my room, my boyfriend fell asleep watching TV. Most nights, when this happened, I was okay with it, because I just wanted him to be with me. I didn't like to be alone. The following day, I would wake him up, so he could go home or to work.

Everything seemed as normal as any other night, but all of a sudden, I heard a loud voice. "Carrie, let him go. He's not good for you; let him go." I was scared to death! I jumped out of my bed and looked underneath it to see if someone was there. There wasn't. I woke up my boyfriend hastily and asked him to go home. He didn't mind, because he was tired. I helped him get his shoes and go. I knew I needed to be alone to figure out what had just happened.

I checked everywhere in the room. I checked my closet, under my bed again, and every area I could. I finally sat on the bed and said aloud, "God, is that you?" I didn't hear anything else. I didn't need to. It just replayed in my mind until I finally obeyed. I understood that I never wanted to hear Him like that again. God's voice was the most frightening thing I'd ever heard. His voice made me tremble and feel fear, but at the same time, it was loving and firm. I don't think I'll ever be able to describe in words the way it made me feel. But I knew God meant business with this command.

Once I finally let my boyfriend go, I became lonely. I was brokenhearted. There were many nights I cried myself to sleep and asked God to hold me. I reached out to Him and asked Jesus to come and be with me. I asked Him to heal my broken heart and comfort me in my loneliness. Every night, I cried and reached out to Him, and He came. I heard His soft, gentle voice tell me, "Carrie, I am here. I will never leave you nor forsake you. I love you, Carrie. I am holding you, and I am combing through your hair. Carrie, I am with you. I am right next to you. I am holding you." Hearing this, I wept in His arms. I didn't understand why I was so lonely, but I knew He was with me. And if He was with me, that was all I needed.

I didn't have many Christian friends. I didn't have many friends from church either, because I was new, and I didn't know many people. I spent many nights at home, weekend after weekend, with my parents and my dog. I worked on paint-by-number crafts, listened to the Christian radio station, and read my Bible. That was my life. It was very different from going out several nights during the week to clubs. I was lonely.

I was so alone that I began to pray for God to bring me some friends. Often I reminded Him that I had given up my boyfriend, who I thought I was going to marry. Could He at least find me some friends—someone I could relate to?

During this time, I had two constant prayers, which I prayed daily: for God to bring me Christ-like friends and that He would save my family.

At night, I started crying out to God for my family. Each night, I wept for them. I wept for my mom, dad, and sister. I couldn't fathom any of them going to hell. I wept, prayed, and asked God to save them. I begged Him each night to not let them perish, but that they would have everlasting life. I asked God for His mercy, like He bestowed onto me.

Soon after this constant prayer, a girl I had a class with in college became a friend of mine. She was from Laplace, Louisiana. She was very gentle and kind. She invited me to her house one weekend to spend the night and go to her youth group. I was ecstatic to have finally found a Christian friend. I immediately said yes.

Her family served God, and I was amazed. It was very different than mine. At the youth group, during praise and worship, a pastor opened the altar and invited everyone down for prayer. I went. I was very burdened about my family.

When I arrived at the altar, a young man laid his hands on my head and said, "You are worried about your family. But God says, 'I will save them. I have heard your cries and your prayers, and I will save them.'" This broke me. This guy didn't know me, but God did. The Holy Spirit told this pastor what to say. The pastor looked at me and said, "Your parents will be saved within three months." I was overwhelmed with joy and couldn't stop crying. I was so excited that I could barely sleep that night. God told me my family would be saved!

Soon, I began to see God moving in the lives of my parents. They began to go to church with me. They were curious and wanted to see what it was all about. This church was very different from the one I grew up going to with my parents. It was more radical. It wasn't as conservative. It was free! The presence of God was very evident in this place. The Word of God was spoken and you could read it for yourself on the large projection screens.

During this time, God strategically placed people in my path to encourage me and help me learn about the Lord. One lady at work took me under her wing and helped explain things that happened to me. She explained questions I had concerning God, Christ, and the Holy Spirit.

I'm not sure the exact date my parents gave their hearts to the Lord. I do, however, have documented in my Bible the first prophetic meeting we went to together on July 15, 2001. It was in Donaldsonville, Louisiana. My friend from work invited my parents and me to hear a prophet at a small church. I was proud and honored we were all going together.

God spoke things through this prophet about my parents that were amazing. He spoke things to me that I knew were inspired by the Holy Spirit. To this day, my mom still professes some of the marvelous things spoken at that meeting.

A few months after I asked God for more Christian friends, a friend of mine from high school got saved during one of the services I attended. I knew she probably felt alone and maybe a little nervous, so as soon as the people at the altar were released to go to the prayer room, I ran up and hugged her. She was excited to see me. We were both happy and crying. I told her I had been coming to this church for about six months, and I was very happy to see her. She introduced me to another girl who was in the youth group and had her own Bible study. This group is where I met a lot of people my age who were in college or working.

In 2005, my sister and her husband gave their hearts to the Lord! During a crusade meeting in Baton Rouge, Louisiana, they both accepted Jesus into their lives. God showed me in 2002 that He was going to use my sister as a mighty intercessor for Him.

God began to teach me about His ways. He began to teach me the Bible through dreams and visions. He would show me a vision, and then I would later find it in His Word. This helped reinforce the vision and assured me that I wasn't losing my mind. It took faith to believe the dreams and visions He showed me. I wouldn't understand most of them right away; I had to ask Him to explain.

Specifically, during our church's corporate fast in January of 2002, God did a deep healing work inside of me. Every time I prayed and sought Him in a quiet place, He poured His love on me so strong that it was almost too much to handle. I wept in His presence for hours at a time. I cried out to Him in utterances I couldn't explain—in my heavenly language I spoke to Him. I didn't want to use my words—I didn't trust my words. I wanted my spirit to talk to His. I wanted the Holy Spirit to communicate with Him and tell Him what I needed.

I cried so hard that my face was swollen from the tears. I was hardly able to see out of my eyes. I spoke for a time, and then I just listened. I waited on the Lord to see if He wanted to speak to me.

As I prayed and fasted, in one particular prayer session, I heard the voice of the Lord very clearly. He said, "Carrie, I want to talk to you about what happened to you that night." The night of my near-death experience was a topic I didn't mind skipping, because it was a strong reality to me. God said, "I was there for you in your darkest hour. Carrie, I was there. Do you remember when you saw nothing but white? You were indeed dying, and if I would have let you die, you would have had to face my great white throne of judgment, and you would have gone to hell. But because of My mercy, I sent forth My warring angels and had them encamped around your emergency room bed. I had one of them mark you to let the Devil know that no longer were you going to serve him, but you were going to serve Me."

At this time in my walk with God, I was a babe in Christ. I had never heard of such a thing. I didn't know there was a great white throne of judgment. What was that? The fact God said there really was a hell shook me to the core.

Were my beliefs wrong for so many years? Was I wrong about hell? Was I wrong to think that I could commit suicide and eventually go to heaven? What else was I wrong about? Did all paths lead to God? Could I be reincarnated, or was that wrong, too? I was blown away! I couldn't believe God would send me to hell! I couldn't believe I was that close to going there!

But God confirmed His message to me, as He had done faithfully so many times. A few months later, I found the Scriptures. When I heard them at church, I almost fell out of my chair during the service. I was blown away that it was all so undoubtedly true!

"Then I saw a great white throne and him who was seated on it. Earth and sky fled from his presence, and there was no place for them. And I saw the dead, great and small, standing before the throne, and books were opened. Another book was opened, which is the book of life. The dead were judged according to what they had done as recorded in the books. The sea gave up the dead that were in it, and death and Hades gave up the dead that were in them, and each person was judged according to what he had done. Then death and Hades were thrown into the lake of fire. The lake of fire is the second death. If anyone's name was not found written in the book of life, he was thrown into the lake of fire." (Revelation 20:11–15).

God told me, "The mark is on your nose. That is why you have a cross on your nose. That is why you felt the peace that surpassed all understanding when you looked up at your IV bag in the emergency room. It was because you had been in the presence of My angels. I was there in your darkest hour. I was right beside you. I have never left you nor forsaken you, Carrie. I have always been there for you. I have heard every prayer, and I have seen every tear. I have carried you. I have never abandoned you, My child. I love you, and you are Mine."

I find great joy in sharing my testimony. I am very thankful for all God has done in my life. I have seen His mighty hand save me and most of my family. I have seen God move mightily in the lives of my grandparents, cousins, aunts, and uncles. One thing is for sure—He is no respecter of persons; He doesn't love one and hate the other. He loves us all the same. And His love isn't anything we can fully comprehend or explain.

I know what God has shown me about His love. It is immeasurable, without limit, and without containment. It is overwhelming and the most wonderful thing you can ever experience. No drug, alcohol, sex, or human being can make you feel as awesome as when you feel His love.

Nothing in this world can satisfy you like God's love. It is the most amazing thing. I have walked through valleys, and I have stood on mountains in my walk with the Lord, and one thing is for sure—in the deepest valleys, He always shows me He is faithful. On the highest mountains, He always shows me He is good. I have been transformed because of His love. I am still being transformed because of His love. Each day is a blessing from Him. Each revelation, dream, and vision is a blessing from Him.

One day in God's house is better than a thousand in the world. I have stumbled, and I have fallen, but a righteous woman gets back up. I have learned that God is for me. He is with me. He is my Savior—my everlasting Father. He is my Prince of Peace. He is my Comforter. He is my God who heals and restores me. He is my God who sees and loves me. He understands me, because He created me. He is my deliverer and my healer. He heals the brokenhearted, and He is close to those who suffer. He sends His angels to protect and watch over us.

God loves us so much that while we were still sinners, He died on a cross for us. He took our sin and shame. And He called this sinner by name and saved me from the flames of judgment. I owe my life to Him.

I am not my own anymore; He has purchased me with the ultimate price. And now I live for Him. I serve Him. My whole house serves Him. My parents serve Him, and they are faithful to God. Each week, they serve the Lord in His house. And I have seen God bless me with a godly husband.

Sometimes, I marvel at how good God is! He has given me an abundant life. He is a very good God. He is a gentleman; He is not forceful. He will come to you if you ask Him; He will come into your heart and into your life. He will come. He will give you peace and joy. He will forgive your sins and heal you. He will restore you. I thank God for my parents, husband, church, and mentors. I thank God for all He has done for me. I thank God that He let me live to serve Him. He gave me hope, a future, and a calling. I found purpose in this life. I found Him.

Turning Points

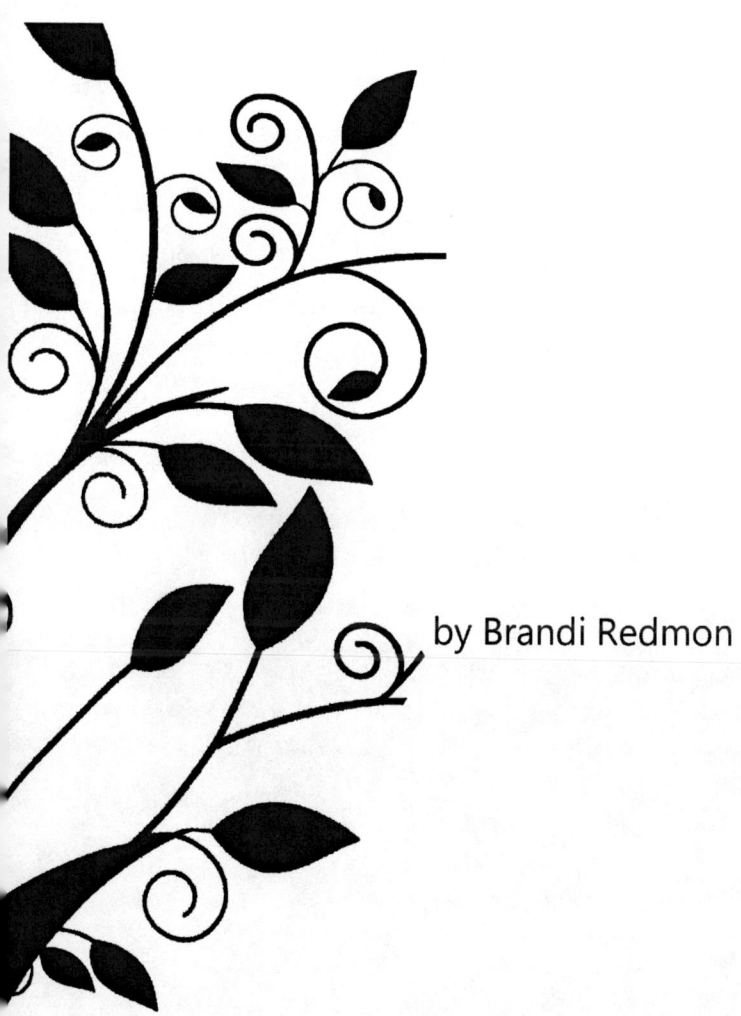

by Brandi Redmon

I had a good life. I married my high school sweetheart and had two beautiful children, a nice house, and job that paid well. My husband, Shane, was my best friend and a wonderful father. I pretty much had it all—or so it seemed. Anyone looking in from the outside would have thought we had the perfect little family, but we—like most people—had our share of problems.

Many of our friends would have been surprised at the numerous battles we were fighting, which seemed almost insurmountable to us at the time. I had considered leaving my husband on several occasions but refused to give up that easily. We persevered and tried to work things out. While in the midst of our struggles and our renewal to make things right, Shane tragically died. My fragmented world officially crumbled.

I became very cold to the people who loved me, and I started to self-destruct. I was still grieving the loss of my sister, who had passed away earlier in the year. I could not understand why this was happening to me. What had I done to deserve so much loss? I began to pick up bad habits that before had appalled me. I was at the point where I didn't care if I lived or died. There were some occasions when I went out, became extremely intoxicated, and then drove home. How did I make it home when I didn't remember driving?

I was angry at everyone. I had a big hole in my heart. I ached and tried just about everything to numb the pain. During all of this mayhem, my parents begged me to go to church with them. I would go occasionally to pacify them. After all of their harassing, I eventually had a regular seat at church. There was something or someone there that I longed to have a relationship with.

"When you pass through the waters, I will be with you; and when you pass through the rivers, they will not sweep over you. When you walk through the fire, you will not be burned; the flames will not set you ablaze" (Isaiah 43:2).

My search continued, and although I hadn't fully surrendered my life to God, I sought Him. I heard other people talk about having a relationship with the Lord, and I longed for that too. One chilly fall day, I was brought a step closer to fulfilling that desire.

My mom and I were Christmas shopping with my daughters. It had been a long morning, and we were all starving. We chose a local café amongst a string of small shops. As we pulled up alongside the curb and were about to exit the car, I noticed a man sitting outside one of the stores. His clothes looked as worn as the lines on his face. I assumed he was homeless. His expression was difficult to distinguish, and I wasn't sure if he was angry or sad. I made sure the girls got out of the vehicle on my side so they wouldn't be near him.

While we were inside the café, this stranger was heavy on my heart. I talked with Mom about my concern for him. When we left the restaurant, he was gone.

A few weeks later, our church was preparing Christmas baskets for families in need. My mom and I went to buy groceries for the baskets. After we finished shopping, we went to eat lunch. The same man was sitting outside the café in the same spot. He had an angry expression on his tired, dirty face. This time, I avoided making eye contact with him as I got out of the car.

All during lunch, I thought about him. I asked Mom what she thought his story was. She responded, "I don't know. Why don't you ask him?" I brushed off the idea; I wouldn't know what to say.

As we walked out of the café, Mom got in the car. My legs, however, did not stop. They continued to walk toward the man. I stood in front of him, frozen for just a moment. I thought of turning away and running to the car, but I could not control my legs. Something had a hold of me and was not letting go!

Finally, I realized I needed to speak. I asked if the man lived in the area. The mean expression on his face disappeared. He said he did and told me his name was Darrell. I asked if he would like a food basket from our church. After he realized my intentions were good, he began to talk with me. He told me he cleaned the parking lot for the entire shopping center every day for $35 a week. That really troubled me.

The previous Sunday, my daddy had given Mom a coat that was too tight for him. It was in the car, as we planned to give it to the church for anyone who needed it. I asked Darrell if he had a coat. "No," he replied.

I told him, "Hold on a second" and got ready to walk back to Mom's vehicle.

Darrell stopped me. "Before you go … can I have $0.25?" I reached into my pocket and pulled out a $5 bill. Without looking to see how much it was, he had already begun to cry. I told him to hold on, and I walked to the car.

I smelled the coat to make sure it was clean; it smelled of Daddy's cologne. I took it to Darrell, and as I handed it to him, tears streamed down his face. He started to approach me to give me a hug but stopped. I reached over and hugged him. His words were soft but clear: "God bless you." I told him I would pray for him.

When I got in the vehicle, Mom was crying. She said when I came to get the coat, she was watching him. He was holding the $5 bill in his hands, looking at it, and rubbing it between his fingers. I turned to look at him; he was sitting down again, still crying. I also wept.

This was my first experience with the Holy Spirit where I recognized He had taken hold of my heart. I was very excited! When I got to church the following Sunday, I shared my experience and asked everyone to keep Darrell in their prayers.

TIME, LOVE, AND CHANGE

The Lord is good. Day by day, He healed my heart. It had been almost four years since the tragic end of my first marriage. I could finally say I had let go of all of the hate and anger I had carried. A wonderful man had entered my world, and the beginning of my new life started on November 28, 2007 when Clay and I were married.

As time went on, I finally realized what it was I had been searching for all those Sunday mornings. I found Him—I found Jesus. I was saved on December 16, 2007, which also happened to be the four-year anniversary of Shane's death. That December morning, everything changed; it was no longer all about me.

"For God so loved the world that he gave his one and only Son, that whoever believes in him shall not perish but have eternal life" (John 3:16).

A short time after being saved, I grew concerned about my past. I was ashamed of the mistakes I had made, and I felt guilty. I still had not truly worked to build a relationship with God. I was afraid. Was everything I had done just for the sake of saying I was saved? I didn't understand how God could love me or how He could send His son to die for me—me and all my terrible mistakes. I began to contemplate these things in my head and heart.

Around April of 2008, I was blessed to meet a man by the name of Cary Gilham who spoke at our church one week. When I heard his testimony, it reminded me of my life. We had gone through many similar experiences. He lost his brother. He dealt with addictions. He dealt with anger.

That night, Cary gave me hope. When he sang "Make My Life a Bible," I knew I needed to change my ways and start living right. My life was nowhere near a Bible! I wasn't living the way God's Word instructs us. I felt the Holy Spirit speaking to me, and I finally knew in my heart that God loved me. I left our church that spring day a changed person.

Sometimes turning our lives around takes hearing a testimony, or God's promises, more than once. Sometimes Christ's message of love takes a while to travel from your head to your heart. Hearing how Cary conquered his problems and let his light shine for Jesus touched me. That day, I too began to live my life for Jesus—to let my light shine for Him.

"For God, who said, 'Let light shine out of darkness,' made his light shine in our hearts to give us the light of the knowledge of the glory of God in the face of Christ" (2 Corinthians 4:6).

On February 12, 2010, Cary died of a heart attack. Everyone in my family had great respect for Cary and the message he brought. After learning of his passing, I put together a video tribute to him and played it during church service on Valentine's Day. Cary was special to me; he played a big role in my life as a new Christian.

That particular Sunday was significant for another reason, too. My family and I had been praying for the salvation of my brother, Brad. Over the previous few months, I talked to him about Jesus, but Brad put up a wall. On occasion, he would make excuses—for instance, he did not want to go in front of the church to give his heart to Jesus in front of everyone. I began to talk to Brad almost all the time about Jesus. Brad sometimes got irritated with me, but I knew he was listening.

At the end of the Valentine's Day service, my brother accepted Jesus Christ as his Lord and Savior.

GOD PROVIDES

The Lord was moving mightily in the lives of my family, and I began to recognize it. That January, my husband, Clay, lost his job due to company layoffs. He was provided a severance package, but with four children, it wasn't enough to make ends meet. We prayed and stood on faith that God would provide. Clay sent resumes, but no one was hiring.

Finally, after a month and a half, Clay went to work! We gave God all the praise and glory, because there was no other explanation. We couldn't believe we were able to live on one month's severance for six weeks.

During this time, our faith grew extremely strong. We continued to tithe to the church and also supported an evangelist who traveled through the area. As blessings showered down on us, we only had God to thank.

Around the same time, I also found myself worrying about finances for the church. As the treasurer, it was my job to make sure all the bills were paid. The small country church didn't have a lot of money. In fact, the church gave most of the money it had back to the community. Typically, however, there were about four months out of the year when the church really struggled.

One Monday morning, I told Pastor Valmon that the church needed $1,200 to pay the beginning of the month's bills. We didn't know where the funds would come from, but God always provided.

That Wednesday evening, at Bible study, I was told a gentleman wanted to speak with me. The man said he had some seed to sow, and he wanted to plant it in fertile ground. I handed him a tithe envelope.

Pastor Valmon and I were in conversation when the gentleman returned the envelope. I glanced at the amount on the outside; it was for the exact amount of $1,200. I looked at my pastor and asked with a grin, "How much money did I tell you we needed?" I showed him the envelope, and he smiled back at me. We prayed with the man, and the presence of the Holy Spirit surrounded us.

"And my God will meet all your needs according to his glorious riches in Christ Jesus" (Philippians 4:19).

BEAUTIFUL CHALLENGE

God can supply our needs in many ways, as I learned through two people very dear to me. Dorothy and Preston, two elderly members of our church, were instrumental in my healing process and spiritual growth. Everyone loved them—especially me.

One Tuesday evening, I received a phone call from Dorothy. She told me that her husband, Preston, was not doing well, and they expected him to pass soon. She said she had been touched by the nice things I said about Preston in the previous weeks, and she asked me to write his eulogy. I was honored—and scared. I knew this would be a huge challenge.

That evening, I began writing my thoughts down to prepare for the eulogy. I struggled. I had many wonderful things in my heart to say about Preston, but nothing worked on paper. I put aside the project with plans to work on it again another time.

The next day, I went to visit Preston in the nursing home. I said a prayer over him and hummed "The Old Rugged Cross," one of his favorite hymns. As I leaned over and kissed him, he had a tear streaming down his cheek. I told Dorothy, "The day he passes will be a beautiful day."

Early Thursday morning, I walked outside. The sun shined, and a gentle breeze blew. I knew the moment the wind brushed my face that Preston had woken up in heaven. Around 7:15 that morning, I received the phone call letting me know Preston had passed.

All week long, I continued to struggle writing the eulogy. It didn't seem to matter what time of day I sat down in front of the computer; nothing flowed. Saturday evening was different. I picked up my laptop and began to type. I had been praying for God to give me the words, and they finally came! I couldn't type fast enough. God answered my prayers and gave me the words to say! Sweeter still was the fact that my dear friend was in our Father's house—having arrived, no less, on a beautiful morning.

Do not let your hearts be troubled. Trust in God; trust also in me. In my Father's house are many rooms; if it were not so, I would have told you. I am going there to prepare a place for you. And if I go and prepare a place for you, I will come back and take you to be with me that you also may be where I am. You know the way to the place where I am going" (John 14:1–4).

That's where I want to go, too—where Jesus is—but I have learned that along the way, there will be critical choices to make. We all have them—turning points in our lives that are clearly of God. Yet sometimes we choose to ignore them and write off the tugging on our hearts as imagination or coincidence. But God is more than we can dare to dream or imagine. He can use absolutely anything for our good. He can use a stranger in the street, the testimony of a believer, or any kind of need in our lives.

Learning to trust in God and to be led by the Holy Spirit is a lifelong journey. I am sure my life will have many more turning points, but as long as I stay close to the Lord, I am reassured—through His love and the salvation Jesus Christ offers—that He will turn things to good.

"And we know that in all things God works for the good of those who love him, who have been called according to his purpose" (Romans 8:28).

Following a Faithful God

by Jeanine Garcia

Disheartened, I crouched in the middle of the grass and gazed across our sprawling backyard. It seemed the weeds had sprung up overnight and completely overtaken my once well-manicured lawn. It was only the end of February, but already the heat and humidity of an impending Louisiana spring caused rivers of sweat to run down my back. Tears began forming and slid silently down my face.

"God, I can't do this anymore," I quietly prayed. "It's too much for me to handle alone." This realization came as quite a shock. Working in my yard had always been a joy, and I would often escape the busyness of life as a wife and mother of three boys to disappear into the peaceful solitude of my garden. But Logan and Benjamin were grown and had moved into apartments of their own. Sam was the only one around to help, and our spacious home and yard were proving to be too much to care for. I heard God's gentle voice whisper, "It's time."

For several months, my hard-working husband had been making comments of discontent regarding his business. He and I planned to eventually rid ourselves of all worldly possessions, buy a dually truck with a fifth wheel, and strike out on the road in full-time worship ministry. In nearly twenty-four years of marriage, Peter rarely complained about anything, and I sensed this time the Lord was the one urging him to move on to the next chapter of our lives. I somehow knew deep in my soul that Peter was right, but I had grown to really love my life in Baton Rouge. We attended a great church, had wonderful friends, and had a beautiful home which we had just spent the last three years remodeling. In fact, the transformation was almost complete ... how could I leave? But as I knelt in the grass on that warm February day, I knew God was calling me to leave it all behind.

Before I could think twice, I grabbed my cell phone and pushed the speed dial. Peter answered, and without even greeting him, I said, "Are you really ready to sell it all and go?"

I could hear him chuckling in relief. "Yes, I am," he replied.

"Then let's do it!" I cried. I had to fully commit before fear began to set in.

It always seemed to work this way in our relationship—God would first speak to Peter, who would mention to me the direction he sensed God leading. I would hear Peter out, panic a little, and for a few weeks ponder the wild plans laid before me. Then, after Peter spent many hours pleading to the Lord for my heart to yield to the Spirit, I would agree. I guess even after walking with Jesus for many years, I still struggled with fear and submission to the plans He had for me.

The next few weeks flew by as we excitedly planned our departure. As I perused our home filled with gorgeous antique furnishings, I realized just how much we had acquired in our lifetime together. Getting rid of it all would be no easy task. We decided to hold our first garage sale the first week of April. I posted an ad online only to realize later it was the Saturday before Easter. We decided to go ahead with it anyway. My friend, Lucy, offered to come stay the night before so we could rise early to set up. At 6:30 a.m., our first customers appeared, and by 7:30, the driveway was filled with people. In my many years of holding yard sales, I could not recall anything quite like the frenzy that Saturday over patio furniture, old tools, and household junk. Lucy seemed to read my thoughts, and with a harried look, she exclaimed, "I have never in all my life seen so many people at a yard sale!"

I knew God was using this sign to confirm to our hearts that we were on the right track. We held sales every weekend until the fourth of July. I watched in amazement as our household goods and furnishings flew out the door. For the most part, people were willing to pay the price we asked for the furniture. As each item left my home, I experienced an incredible feeling of freedom, like a heavy burden was being lifted from my shoulders. One lady bought our beautiful iron bed, so afterward; we simply put the mattress on the floor and slept there.

People asked us where we were moving, and as we shared our plans with them, many said, "Oh, we're believers, too!" They were very excited about what God was doing in our lives, and many agreed to pray for us. By July of 2009, we were living with only the bare necessities. I quickly came to realize how strangely peaceful and content I became with so little in the house. In a society which seems to always be striving for abundance as well as the latest invention, I experienced what Paul learned in Philippians 4:11: *"I am not saying this because I am in need, for I have learned to be content whatever the circumstances."* What a wonderful state in which to exist!

Soon after Independence Day, my husband and I prepared to embark on a road trip to Saskatchewan, Canada for my family reunion. We charted a course from Baton Rouge to the reunion and then planned to make our way down to New Mexico to visit Peter's family, with some scheduled ministry stops along the way. Our middle son, Benjamin, had left a week prior to attend a three-day concert in Michigan. His plan was to visit the family farms in Manitoba before the reunion officially started. My cousin called. She had not heard from Ben and was growing worried. At the time, Benjamin had been running from God and the calling on his life for a couple of years. He had become involved in drugs and alcohol.

The phone rang on a sultry Tuesday afternoon. "Mrs. Garcia?" said a friendly voice. "I am calling from the state trooper's office here in Crystals Falls, Michigan." My heart sank, and my stomach lurched. "Your son has been arrested for possession of illegal weapons." The trooper proceeded to tell me the story of my son's reckless driving and subsequent accident, search of the vehicle, and finally, his arrest. Benjamin was charged with two felonies and one misdemeanor for possession of a very impressive knife collection. Even though Ben was running from God, he was one of the kindest and gentlest people I knew, and the most violent thing he had ever done with the knives was slice an apple.

A few nights later, I tossed and turned in my bed, incapable of sleep. Although the Lord gave me assurance that everything was happening according to His plan, I longed to hear Ben's voice—to tell him that we loved him, the Lord loved him, and we were praying for him. Suddenly, the thought popped into my mind, *I wonder if there's a Calvary Chapel close by?*

My husband and I had been part of Calvary Chapel churches for over twenty years, and one thing I knew about this family of churches across the United States was the bond of fellowship and willingness to help each other in times of need. The next morning, I checked online for a Calvary Chapel, praying I could find one within a reasonable driving distance. I hoped to find someone who would be willing to minister to Benjamin. I typed in the name of the town where Ben was arrested, and up popped a church fifteen miles away! I was soon to learn that our son was arrested in the only town in the entire Upper Peninsula of Michigan that had a Calvary Chapel. Peter immediately called Pastor Bill, using the number on the website. Within days, guys from the church were at the jail, visiting and loving on Ben. The church also had a home for wayward young men called the Brother's House, and Pastor Bill informed us that as soon as Ben was released from jail, he would have a bed at the house.

I visited the website from Calvary Chapel Iron River, and I saw several pictures of young men playing guitars and worshipping God. They all had long hair, dreadlocks, tattoos, or a combination of all three, and they looked just like Ben! Ben, our hippie son, had always stood out like a sore thumb in Baton Rouge. But I could see he would fit in with this group of kids. I was filled with inescapable joy, knowing deep in my heart this was a powerful move of God on behalf of my son and the answer to many hours of prayer by us.

"The prayer of a righteous man is powerful and effective" (James 5:16b).

Our route to Canada had changed. We decided to go to Michigan first and see Ben. When we arrived at the jail, there sat our middle son, looking humiliated behind the glass window. He was teary, and his eyes would not meet his father's gaze. He was still fairly hard-hearted. He still had an agenda for his life and held on to the plans he had made. But we could tell something had changed, because he listened and considered the words of advice we gave. We left Michigan encouraged but praying more fervently than ever. We knew Ben's life hung in the balance between two very real spiritual worlds.

We ventured on, continuing our vacation across the beautiful country.

As we led worship at several churches in three different states, we could sense that we were definitely doing what God was calling us to do; we were right in the center of His hand and will.

We had been on the road, living out of suitcases for two and a half weeks, and I looked forward to getting home. The immediate plan was to finish liquidating our belongings and get our house ready to sell. One morning, after we had spent our usual time in prayer together, Peter said to me, "I think we need to go back to Michigan for Ben's court date." Now, I deeply love my son, but at the time, we were approximately sixty miles from the Mexican border. The thought of making the thirty-hour drive back to the Upper Peninsula of Michigan was almost more than I could bear. I knew we had to pray. As we did, the Lord confirmed that seeing Ben was exactly what we needed to do.

When we arrived back in Iron River, we found a very different Benjamin. He was virtually glowing from within, and there was a sweet peace and joy in his countenance. He laughed and joked with the other inmates and some of the guards. He had totally surrendered his life back to the Lord! He told us he was content to remain in jail, and if God saw fit to release him, he'd be glad. But he was fully ready to accept God's will for his life and the consequences of his actions. He was still incarcerated when we left, but thanks to the Lord, he was released after forty-one days, and the charges were reduced to very minimal ones. God's faithfulness once again shined through the darkest of circumstances!

During the drive back to Michigan, my husband and I received a call from Baton Rouge. It was from a friend of our son, Logan. She had called to inform us that Logan was in jail in the East Baton Rouge Parish prison! Several weeks prior to this, I had a long phone conversation with Logan. He had called to tell me that the still, small voice of God had begun to speak to him about the person he had become. He had taken a long, hard look in the mirror and was repulsed by what he saw.

Logan had a long and involved history with alcohol and just about every drug imaginable. He had drawn near to God many times in his life, but every time, the fear of completely surrendering would cause him to run away. So as Logan once again surveyed his life and the path he was on, he drew near to the Lord, became filled with fear, and began to run back to drugs and alcohol. This time, his run resulted in him being arrested for stealing something small from a pharmacy. It was almost as if the Lord put His hand out and said, "You're done. No more running."

The night of Logan's arrest, he was with a friend who had recently given her heart to the Lord. She was a long-time friend of Logan's and had witnessed firsthand his running from God. She told me she wasn't going to bail him out; she felt Logan needed to stay in jail. She sensed Logan needed some time in prison so God could speak to him without distraction. I agreed.

Peter, Sam, and I arrived back home to Baton Rouge one week after Logan's arrest. Our priority was to go visit Logan in jail. We piled in the car and made the trek across town, only to be turned away. The prison had a very strict dress code of which we were unaware. Peter and Sam both were dressed in shorts, and I had on flip-flops. The rules were understandable, but we were discouraged nonetheless. Peter had taken off from work that Wednesday, as it was the only day visitors were permitted. We would have to wait an entire week before we could see Logan.

As we painstakingly walked across the parking area, heads hung low beneath a warm Louisiana sun, a van turned in to the visitor lot. Our rejection must have been apparent, because the van slowly pulled beside me, and a woman rolled down her window. She asked if we had tried to visit a prisoner but had been turned away. I told her that we had. She explained that the same thing happened to her on a previous visit, and this time, she had brought extra clothing to ensure admittance. She offered to lend me some clothes. "Yes!" I jumped at the chance. I was given a pair of closed-toed shoes and an overshirt to cover my shoulders, which were exposed by the tank top I was wearing. My outfit looked ridiculous, but that did not matter. I was going to see my son!

"Now to him who is able to do immeasurably more than all we ask or imagine, according to his power that is at work within us, to him be glory in the church and

in Christ Jesus throughout all generations, for ever and ever! Amen" (Ephesians 3:20–21).

Logan had known about God all his life. We raised him in church. I was pregnant with him when Peter and I first attended and then began leading worship at Calvary Chapel in Oxnard California, our home for many years. He had known of the Lord and heard His Word, but all those years, Logan tried to walk with the Lord through the knowledge he had in his head. I believe that is why he continued to stumble. Doing the right thing wasn't enough. Logan had never quite let the love of the Lord travel the eighteen inches from his head to his heart. For years, I told him that one day, it would reach his heart. How I hoped the day of my visit was that day.

I soon realized my attire was only the first of many requirements I would need to fulfill in order to obtain a visitor pass. I had paperwork to complete and checkpoints to cross before finally being approved. A guard led me down a long corridor into a circular room with a guard station. The room was filled with small windows, many with awaiting faces on the other side. I slowly began to walk past each cubby, searching for the face of my oldest child.

When I sat down across from Logan, the thick pane of glass between us seemed of no consequence. I was relieved to see him, even under the circumstances. His hair was unkempt and dirty. I didn't blame him for being too afraid to shower. Tears began to flow as we sat silently and looked into each other's eyes. His face glowed, and he smiled broadly through his tears. "Oh, Mom, I started reading Matthew, and when I got to the part about the crucifixion …" He paused. "When I got to the part about the crucifixion, I had to put the covers over my head to finish reading it. I cried for twenty minutes. It never impacted me like that before!" More tears streamed down my face, and I knew that day was the day. He got it, and this time, it was real. My heart was rejoicing!

Eleven days after Logan was arrested, his friend called my cell phone. She said she felt like the Holy Spirit had spoken to her, and it was time to bail him out. Bailing Logan out of jail was not an option for us. We had always told our boys that if they ever got arrested to call us. We would love to talk with them, but that they would be held responsible for their own actions. We would not bail them out. We had to live this out. We couldn't afford to bail both boys out, and we couldn't bail one out and not the other. We stood firm on our word, and neither asked us to change it.

Ben was in jail for forty-one days and Logan for eleven. Their experiences were as different as their personalities, but our amazing God used the same circumstance—imprisonment—to bring them both to Himself.

"And we know that in all things God works for the good of those who love him, who have been called according to his purpose" (Romans 8:28).

Within a week of Logan's release, he left for a Christian drug rehabilitation program in Tennessee, and when he returned to Baton Rouge, he found a home church. He immediately felt comfortable and connected to his new church family, and he began to seek and serve the Lord.

In early September, we sold Peter's work vehicle and purchased a dually to pull the fifth wheel we eventually planned to buy. We were also working on home projects: garage sales, finishing touches to our home, and things of the sort. But much to our dismay, Peter's business was suddenly dry. He did not get a single job through his otherwise steady handyman business. I started to feel a twinge of panic. Peter decided to embrace his lack of contract jobs and spend the next two weeks working on our kitchen—the last room of our home to be redone. We redid all the cabinetry and painted. Immediately after our kitchen was finished, he received a phone call, and the work began to flow again. This length of dry spell had never happened in his business, but it was just what we needed to complete the work on our house.

We placed a "For Sale by Owner" sign in the yard. A few interested lookers came by and viewed the house, but we had no buyers. Christmas came and went, and still no offers. In January of 2010, we listed the house on the internet. We were ready. Almost all of our furniture and personal belongings were sold. What remained were things we used, planned to put into storage, or planned take with us. Time passed, but things did not happen as quickly as we expected. We continued to weed through what was left of our belongings while our house stayed on the market.

Then it happened. One spring afternoon, we got a phone call that would eventually change the way I viewed the next chapter of our lives. Some friends at church needed to move from Baton Rouge to Missouri, but they were unable to afford a moving truck, so they called us. Without hesitation, we agreed to help, and within the next few days, we packed our truck and a small trailer with their belongings and headed to Missouri. After settling them in their new home, we were back on the road headed to South Carolina for a wedding of some friends.

We passed through Tennessee, where we stopped at a little church and led worship. We went on faith, knowing we would not be able to afford a hotel but not wanting to pass up an opportunity to fulfill our calling. We had no idea where we would stay, but the Lord provided housing and blessed us with the opportunity to stay in the home of a church family for the few days we were there. We arrived in South Carolina and enjoyed the wedding and some additional ministry opportunities. To our delight, we were provided great accommodations in the form of a lake house for three days. The home was relaxing and beautiful and provided a much-needed time of rest for us.

As we traveled to various cities and churches, we were amazed as we watched God open up housing for us. We met people and were given a chance to really get to know them. We weren't tucked away somewhere in a fifth wheel by ourselves. We fellowshipped, made new friends, and encouraged one another with the love of God. As we headed back to Baton Rouge, Peter and I began to talk about how the trip had unfolded. We had been blessed with guest rooms and lake houses, new friends, and genuine people displaying the love of God to us. We were able to minister to them in more ways than through our music; we were face-to-face in their homes, and it was awesome! The Lord showed us that this was His plan all along. There was to be no fifth wheel. We were supposed to pack up and go immediately! I knew it was God, because this way of traveling was the complete opposite of what I had planned, yet He was able to change my heart to choose His will over mine. He never ceases to amaze me.

"For the eyes of the Lord range throughout the earth to strengthen those whose hearts are fully committed to him" (2 Chronicles 16:9a).

Upon returning to Baton Rouge, we sold a few more pieces of furniture and began to re-sort and pack. We boxed up items I had originally thought would be part of our necessities in the fifth wheel. These things were now intended for storage in our house, which we still owned, in California. Our renters, who were old friends from church, were happy to give us the unused attic space. As I packed, thoughts of how our house note in Baton Rouge would be paid flitted across my mind. That old, familiar fear began to creep into my heart. I was immediately reminded of Paul's words in Philippians 4:19: *"And my God will meet all your needs according to his glorious riches in Christ Jesus."* They were great words of comfort, and as I chose to take God at His Word, my fears were put to rest. We loaded up a trailer and the truck bed with all our remaining worldly possessions and left our home. We were officially on the road. It was July of 2010.

We traveled through New Mexico, visited with Peter's family, and then went to California to unload the trailer. We then went on to Michigan for Ben's birthday in August. God opened up doors for us to lead worship in many churches along the way. We were in our new phase of life—traveling. We watched God provide for our every need.

Beginning the first of September, our home in Baton Rouge was rented to some friends from church. We had only gone one month without a renter, and God miraculously provided for our house payment. Have you ever tried to balance your budget and noticed it didn't work on paper, yet all your bills were paid? That's God at work! It doesn't have to make sense, but He always provides—even if it's not what we thought the plan was going to be.

Leaving our home with no renter and no income was a huge step of faith for me. It was easier, though, than you might think. I had seen God be faithful to us through the years. And as long as you know you are in God's will, you can trust Him.

I am very thankful for how God worked everything out. The Lord rescued my sons out of the world and brought them back to walking with Him. I was able to leave home and enjoy the ministry God was calling us to, knowing my two older boys were safe in His arms, even though I couldn't touch them from multiple states away.

"In his heart a man plans his course, but the Lord determines his steps" (Proverbs 16:9).

God has shown me that when He wants me to step out in faith, it's okay to make a plan. But I have to be willing for His plan to override mine. I have learned that as long as I am open to the leading of the Lord and walk in His will, things will always work out for the best. It has been exactly one year since we left Baton Rouge, and life on the road has been thrilling and satisfying. Every need I have had—whether spiritual, emotional, or physical—has been met in abundance.

"'For I know the plans I have for you,' declares the Lord, 'plans to prosper you and not to harm you, plans to give you hope and a future'" (Jeremiah 29:11).

God has been more than faithful!

Sacrificing Isaac

by Emily Billings

Have you ever felt like God was not pleased with you—like He was waiting for you to mess up so He could punish you? I used to believe that if I made a mistake, God would whop me on the head. I figured that as a Christian, I should know better; I shouldn't mess up or sin. I felt like my Christian walk was strictly about performance, and God would reward me accordingly.

It seemed God only loved me and was pleased with me when I did well. I never knew how much of the Bible I was to read in a day or how long I should pray; nothing felt good enough. How much would God find acceptable? If I didn't read the Bible in the morning, I would go through the entire day obsessed with the thought, *I need to read!* Grace and unconditional love were foreign concepts to me. In a sense, I was afraid of grace.

Because of what I heard growing up in church, I felt as if grace was an unsafe subject. I honestly believed grace would cause me to slip into sin. I was scared I would feel like it was okay for me to mess up and then end up living a sinful life. After hearing sermons (no matter how positive), I would find something from the sermon with which to condemn myself. If I did not feel guilty after leaving a church service, it must have meant my heart was becoming hard. I expected to leave church feeling bad about myself.

I felt rejected by God and most people. No matter how many people told me, "God loves you," I refused to accept it. I only thought about all the sin I had willingly involved myself in and wondered how God could possibly want me.

In 2006, I felt God drawing me to go to the St. Louis Dream Center for an internship program. I first saw an article about the internship in *Enjoying Everyday Life*, the magazine from Joyce Meyer Ministries. It was a nine-month program that focused on inner-city evangelism to the homeless and children. I was working a full-time job and finishing my bachelor's degree in sociology. My heart's desire was to be a social worker, so this internship seemed right up my alley—if I could actually work up the nerve to go.

I had also begun to develop a relationship with a guy from church, Craig. He was calling me, and we were hanging out together. In November of 2006, we had a serious discussion regarding our relationship. He knew I was thinking of going out of state for the internship, and it made him hesitant to seriously date me. Yet we liked each other very much and wanted a deeper relationship. He decided to continue dating me. I graduated from college in December of 2006, and Craig asked me to be his official girlfriend in January of 2007. If I went to St. Louis, it wouldn't be until August.

Over time, Craig and I grew closer and fell in love with each other. I debated doing the internship. I sent out letters, asking people I knew for financial support. I figured if God wanted me to go, He would provide. And provide He did! I ended up with more than enough for the cost of the program and had plenty to live on while there. Someone paid my car insurance for six months, and another person paid my cell phone bill for nine months! It was obvious to everyone around me that God meant for me to go. However, the closer it got to August, the more confused I became.

I was afraid of leaving Craig. He was my first boyfriend, and I didn't want to lose him. He loved me for me and seemed serious about staying with me. Craig claimed he would not date anyone else while I was in St. Louis. He claimed he would wait for me, but deep down, I didn't believe him.

Then there was my dog. I hated the thought of parting with him, though I knew he would be safe with my family. Moving away for nine months meant I had to give up my job, income, family, friends, and home church. The fact that I do not like change didn't make the thought of leaving any easier. Most painful of all, though, was the thought of separating from Craig.

Some time later God tested Abraham. He said to him, "Abraham!" "Here I am," he replied. Then God said, "Take your son, your only son, Isaac, whom you love, and go to the region of Moriah. Sacrifice him there as a burnt offering on one of the mountains I will tell you about." Early the next morning Abraham got up and saddled his donkey. He took with him two of his servants and his son Isaac. When he had cut enough wood for the burnt offering, he set out for the place God had told him about" (Genesis 22:1–3).

I felt like Abraham—like God was asking me to give up more than I could imagine. Unlike Abraham, though, I did not fully trust God or understand His goodness. That was one of the reasons I was scared to obey Him; I was scared to let go. Part of me was also scared of disobeying Him—that if I didn't go, He would punish me. I had always been drawn to inner-city ministry, so I believed that is why the internship interested me so much. Years later, however, I would be able to see that God had me interested in it for an entirely different reason.

As an intern, I would not be allowed to date—even long-distance. I would be allowed only one five-minute phone call a day to someone of the opposite sex who was not a relative. I felt like I was close to what I had wanted most in life—marriage to a man of my dreams—and I was being asked to give him up. It was not fair! Even with all these conflicting emotions, I knew I had to give the internship a try. I didn't want to pass it up and always wonder "what if."

When it was time to move, Craig and my brother, Ben, drove to St. Louis with me. We took my car. The guys would fly back. It was a bittersweet time. While we enjoyed sightseeing, there was the ever-present thought in the back of my mind that in a few short days, Craig and I would be apart for who knows how long. On the first day of the internship, I brought Craig and Ben to the airport. Thankfully, Ben gave us a few minutes alone. I openly cried, while Craig held back tears. I felt like I was being ripped open—like my heart was being torn out. I cried all that day and almost every day I was there.

The internship workload was pretty tough, consisting of early morning prayer, classes, and then work in the afternoon and ministry on the weekends, but I did not mind. I was able to get my mind off being over six hundred miles away from Craig. And I truly enjoyed the classes and ministry. There were several times, though, when I seriously thought about hopping into my car and leaving for good—when I felt I could not take being separated from Craig any longer. The pain was there every time I thought about him, which was often.

For holidays, I was allowed to go home. I was able to see Craig, but each time, it was harder to return to the internship when the break ended. It felt like my heart was being ripped open again.

I was advised to take advantage of my time in St. Louis, because it would probably be the only time in my life when I could focus solely on my relationship with God. Part of me believed if I left prematurely, God would punish me—that I would have a terrible accident on the way home and maybe die.

I remember on January 4, 2008, shortly after returning to St. Louis from Christmas break, I wanted to leave very badly. The trip home had been my longest since August. I was sitting on the floor in my bedroom, crying, when I opened up a devotional book I was reading at the time. That day's devotional talked about how many people are not willing to leave the comfort and safety of where they are in order to go to where God has called them. I knew God was speaking to me through the book.

I thoroughly enjoyed the street ministry, homeless outreach, and the children's ministry. During my internship, I kept praying, "God, do whatever You want to do in me and through me. Do not let me miss out on anything You have for me!" Throughout the length of my stay in St. Louis, I was bombarded with devotionals on finding out who I was in Christ—finding my identification in Him. We learned how to see God as a loving father. Through classes, prayer time, and personal counseling, I slowly received a revelation of God's love and grace for me. I learned to rest in Him, accept myself, and see myself as being *in Christ*.

I was first saved when I was six years old, but I rededicated my life to God when I was twenty-three. I was in the church the whole time— sometimes serious about my relationship with God and sometimes not. Five years after my rededication, the concept of grace was finally sinking in. Thank God He did not stop pursuing me! Thank God He was so patient with me! God was not mad at me. He was very pleased with me. Even when I messed up, He still loved me—I was still His child. He did not disown me.

"My dear children, I write this to you so that you will not sin. But if anybody does sin, we have one who speaks to the Father in our defense—Jesus Christ, the Righteous One. He is the atoning sacrifice for our sins, and not only for ours but also for the sins of the whole world" (1 John 2:1–2).

I was finally able to see God as a loving father who only wanted the best for me and had good things planned for my life!

"How great is the love the Father has lavished on us, that we should be called children of God! And that is what we are" (1 John 3:1).

At the end of my nine-month internship, Craig and my brother came to see me graduate. Craig really did wait for me! A little over a month after I moved back home, Craig proposed. Nine months later, we were married.

"And we know that in all things God works for the good of those who love him, who have been called according to his purpose" (Romans 8:28).

I can now see that God had me do the internship not only for what I was able to do for others, but also for what He was able to do for me. I gained a correct view of grace. An understanding of grace in its truest sense will lead you to a lifestyle of holiness, not down a pathway of sin. Grace is God's unmerited favor in our lives. Grace is also God's power within us to do whatever He has called us to do and the power to choose holiness over sin.

The more you know and believe in God's love for you, the less you will want to do anything that displeases Him and the more you will desire to live in purity and not wish to hurt His heart. Not everyone has to go through an internship to learn this. Not everyone is as hard-headed as I was. It blows my mind when I think of the measures God will take to win us to Himself and show how much He loves us!

If you have trouble believing God is good and that He loves you unconditionally, I would like to suggest, as was recommended to me, that you read Romans through Hebrews and meditate on all the verses containing the phrases "in Him" and "through Him." And this is my prayer for you:

So *that Christ may dwell in your hearts through faith. And* I *pray that you, being rooted and established in love, may have power, together with all the saints, to grasp how wide and long and high and deep is the love of Christ, and to know this love that surpasses knowledge—that you may be filled to the measure of all the fullness of God"* (Ephesians 3:17–19).

Uprooted and In a Wilderness

by Sandra Mizell

I was a long way from home, walking out of a wilderness experience only the Lord could take me through. Doors of opportunity in Georgia were closing at every front. The Blessing Place, a small church that my husband and I started with a handful of people, was folding up—and we knew it. An unspoken difficulty in our ministry had also begun to surface. My husband, Garlin, and I were accustomed to ministering separately, but this season of ministering together had proven difficult. There seemed to be an undeclared feeling of competition between us, and I didn't know how to handle it.

One day, I cried out to God, "Lord, what do you want us to do?" I had prostrated myself on the floor, my face in the carpet. When I say I cried out to God, I mean that I bawled, howled, had tears spurting out of my eyes like a faucet, and was slinging snot—crying out to God.

In the middle of my wailing session, the phone began to ring. Between my sniffling and coughing, I managed, "Hello." Much to my surprise, a pastor friend of ours from Dover, Ohio was on the other end of the line, asking if I was okay. His next words shook me to the core. He wanted to know if Garlin and I were ready to move up north to help with his church.

Garlin called him back later that evening and agreed we would come for a visit during the New Year holiday. Meanwhile, we would pray and seek God's direction. We wanted to obey the Lord and do what He desired.

After making our visit to Dover, we came home with the idea that if we sold our house in six months, we would move. Our house sold the very next week.

"But he brought his people out like a flock; he led them like sheep through the desert" (Psalm 78:52).

January is a really cold time in Ohio, but by the fifteenth of the month, we had uprooted ourselves from a beautiful home located in the hilly part of Powder Springs, Georgia and moved to New Philadelphia, a neighboring town of Dover. We had accepted the call to help the small church in a lay capacity. We thought that was the reason for our move, but we soon learned the Lord was more interested in doing a work in our lives.

Not knowing what God had in store for us, we quickly felt as though we were in a wilderness. Although wilderness times are not fun; they are usually a place of learning. If you open yourself up to the Spirit of God, He can teach you during these times. Once my husband and I were in Dover, we knew we needed to learn fast. As time passed, we soon became discontented and homesick. We wanted out; we wanted to go home—back to our original home in Baton Rouge, Louisiana as soon as possible. We were ready for whatever the Lord would give us next.

This wilderness, however, took five months. My husband and I both worked secular jobs. This was not necessarily a bad thing, but it was somewhat discomforting, as neither of us liked the type of work we were doing. Garlin took a job selling insurance, and I worked as a secretary for a paneling manufacturer. My job at the factory was not hard work. The people were friendly and helpful, but the environment was a little dusty.

One afternoon, I came home with a bad headache and didn't know what to do about it. I hadn't found a doctor yet and didn't have any medicine to knock out the pain. Lying on the bed, I saw the commercial massage unit given to us by a chiropractor friend. It was designed for use on sore muscles, but I decided to try it on my head. I placed the unit on my neck and shoulders, rubbing and massaging them, and then down my forehead using a back-and-forth motion. I was surprised at how quickly the pain left. My headache was gone. I would have to remember this; it was better than taking medicine.

I went into the living room and sat in my recliner across from Garlin, who was reading the daily newspaper. He didn't notice me at first, but within minutes, he looked over and said, "Baby, are you all right?"

"Yes," I replied. "That massager really worked. My headache is completely gone."

Garlin continued reading the paper, so I asked for part of it. He looked at me again and asked, "What's wrong with your face?"

"What do you mean, what's wrong with my face?" I asked.

He answered, "Your eyes look like they are on the side of your head, and you have this lump on your forehead like a Star Wars character." I jumped up, looked at myself in the mirror, and almost screamed. I did look like one of the Star Wars characters! I had a lump on my forehead, and the bridge of my nose was so swollen that it made my eyes appear to be set on the side of my head. Horrified, I thought I was dying. I didn't know what was happening. I didn't have any pain, but I was badly deformed.

Not knowing where the hospital was in town, Garlin had me lie down and began to pray over me. I joined in. I definitely didn't want to stay looking like that. I had scared myself in the mirror, and I wasn't interested in scaring anyone else. The Lord heard our prayers, and within a few days, my face returned to its normal state. Thank God! Needless to say, I don't recommend using a commercial massage unit on your head.

A couple of weeks later, a dear friend of ours graduated from Rhema Bible Training Center. My husband and I, along with two other couples, were invited to attend. Our short getaway to Tulsa, Oklahoma was a welcome break. We had a wonderful time with our friends. It was like having a reunion; all of us gathered together to celebrate what God was doing in our lives.

On the trip back to Ohio, Garlin and I discussed what happened in Tulsa and how ready we were to get back to Baton Rouge. Leaving the airport in a pouring rain, we started back to our home in New Philadelphia.

As we traveled along the interstate that evening, we talked about what God was doing, wondering what He had for us next. All of a sudden, a red sports car darted from out of nowhere, almost hitting the driver's side mirror. The red car had lost control. It began hydroplaning in front of our Jeep at about sixty-five miles per hour. The car came across the front of our vehicle, almost hit the guard rail, and then skidded back in front of us again only inches away from our front bumper. The car was so close to us that we saw the whites of the driver's eyes—an amazing sight in the blackness of night. The car slid past us at close range three times. When we were about to crash, I screamed, "Jesus!" I felt like a hand came out from heaven, picked up the red car, and threw it in the ditch on the side of the road. It was raining so hard that it took us a while to get back to the sports car. We pulled over to make sure the driver was okay. I rolled down my window to speak to him, but like a bat out of hell, he raced out of the ditch and sped away.

Garlin and I cried, sang, and laughed all the way home. Our God had delivered us! If He had not picked up the sports car and thrown it in the ditch, I wouldn't be able to write about the amazing miracle God had done. After having such a close call with death, we realized we had come to Dover for a specific lesson, and we had already learned it.

Two weeks prior to our short getaway, a leader in the church had taught a course on the four faces of God and the four faces of man. The course changed the way my husband and I saw each other. At the end of the lesson, we each completed a personality profile. God wanted us to understand that we were wired differently, had totally unique personalities, and were designed to complement each other rather than compete against each other. There it was—the competition thing, finally exposed.

Garlin's personality was identified as the man-ox. This personality type prefers to deal with people in an individual, low-pressure, stress-free position. On the other hand, mine was identified as the lion-eagle. This persona was defined as task-oriented, typical of one who critiques everything, more domineering, and aggressive. Having the eagle personality, I could see things further down the road in advance of my husband. Garlin wasn't typically able to see things as far ahead because of his Ox personality; he had his head to the grindstone, working.

Garlin and I saw that God had intentionally designed our personalities to harmonize with one another, like separate instruments in an orchestra. Our ministry together was more valuable to the body of Christ than if we remained soloists. God had meant for us to minister together so we could strengthen other couples. What a revelation—and what freedom! Through this training, we received a valuable impartation, and the Lord wanted us to share this truth with others.

Unknowingly, Garlin and I had already begun to share our knowledge. On the trip to Tulsa, we shared with our friends many of the things we had learned. We passed our knowledge on to them.

At last, we knew why we came to Ohio. We received essential information that would be instrumental in our future ministry together. We both experienced a release; our path had been cleared, and we could go home. The next week, we moved to Baton Rouge. We were uprooted again. We came out of the wilderness by and through the miraculous, saving power of God. The Lord was doing a new thing in our lives.

"See, I am doing a new thing! Now it springs up; do you not perceive it? I am making a way in the desert and streams in the wasteland" (Isaiah 43:19).

Like finding a treasured hidden stream in the desert, it had sprung up un-expectantly—a close call with death and a teacher who taught us powerful lessons. My husband and I received lessons about working together as a couple, depending on each other's strengths, and helping in areas of weakness—all skills required to walk through a wilderness. But the biggest discovery we encountered was that during difficult times—times when we felt we were looking for the right direction but not sure which way to turn to find it—even in these times, we were still led and taught by the Lord. We learned these lessons while walking through our own wilderness, with God guiding our every step.

I Am Available to You

by Peggy Taylor

I can hear their voices clearly—the voices of the evangelists whose programs aired every Sunday morning on television, each with their own catchy songs and phrases.

Growing up, many things were routine—roast on Sundays, red beans and rice on Mondays, meatballs on Thursdays, and dinner served at 5:00. My family always ate meals together. Most people in those days had a tradition of preparing Sunday dinner on Saturday, and our home was no exception.

Other things were routine as well, such as watching my mother starch and iron our Sunday clothes. There were seven of us, and each Saturday, she prepared our clothes. She also pressed Daddy's shirt, handkerchief, and boxers along with her choir robe.

Sundays were devoted to all-day church services. We began with Sunday school, which was followed by a morning service, and then we took a break for dinner. We would return in the late part of the afternoon for Bible study and evening services.

Our TV only aired the Christian station on Sundays—house rules. We didn't mind; in fact, as we readied ourselves for services, we would listen for the familiar sayings. We could hardly wait to hear Evangelist Oral Roberts say those inspiring words—the ones we would all say with him—"Something good is going to happen to you, this very day."

In the evenings, I would listen to my parents' radio. I remember one program's introductory song that gave glory to the name of God. All of these influences helped to shape my optimistic outlook and unquestionable faith in God.

I thank my dad, who went to be with the Lord when I was twelve, and my mother, who steadfastly continued, for being godly examples and raising us to love the Lord. I thank them for their diligence and obedience to the Word, fulfilling Proverbs 22:6, which says: *"Train up a child in the way he should go: and when he is old, he will not depart from it"* (KJV).

I am thankful for order, discipline, and Christian television. We are not only what we eat, but also what we see and hear. Romans 10:17 says, *"So then faith cometh by hearing, and hearing by the word of God"* (KJV).

When I first gave my life to Christ, there was—and still is—a tradition of steps to be fulfilled at our church. The first is baptism—immersion under the water. Then the right hand of fellowship is given when other members of the church come to shake your hand and welcome you into the family of God. Next is your first communion, where you are given a sip of grape juice and a piece of bread. This represents the blood and the body of our Lord and Savior, Jesus Christ. The last requirement is to stand before the congregation and state your determination as a Christian. We stated our determination once every month before taking communion again. The kids always said the same thing; we would help each other memorize it. It went something like this: "My determination is to make heaven my home, and I ask each one of you to pray for me as I pray for you while God fights my battle."

Since my youth and the renewal of my relationship with God, my determination has changed. The Lord revealed to me that in order for me to be used by Him, I first had to have a desire to serve Him and then be obedient to His Word. Thus, my statement has changed to this: "My determination is to be obedient to God's Word, and I ask that you pray for me, and I'll pray for you."

My desire was always there—to be used by God—but oftentimes God puts us to the test. He wants total allegiance to Him. Jesus says in Matthew 10:33, *"But whosoever shall deny me before men, him will I also deny before my Father which is in heaven"* (KJV). We have to speak up and let others know who we are and whose we are.

THE TICKET

This all ties in with a story about a speeding ticket I was issued. My husband seemed to remind me each morning, as I left for work, to be mindful of the school zones. Of course, I appreciated his concern, but I had never received a ticket in my life and had no plans of getting one. Well, you know what happened; I got a ticket—and yes, it was in a school zone. I did not tell my husband. My concern was not because he would be angry or say "I told you so"—he would never do that. He is fortunate to have a calm spirit and not have an angry bone in his body when it comes to me. I just didn't want to confess it to him. You can call that pride.

I did, however, tell everyone at work. The consensus was that a school zone ticket was the worst. It could cost me up to $300. I was nervous. I made arrangements for my sister to accompany me to traffic court on the scheduled date. When we arrived at the ticket office, there were at least twenty people ahead of us. Each had a ticket of some other sort; no one else had one for speeding in a school zone.

There was quite a bit of conversation happening regarding how much each person owed and how he or she would pay. Everyone joked about my ticket. One man wanted to read it. I obliged, and when he looked at it, he noticed something strange. Nowhere on my ticket did it say anything about a school zone. It just said I was going thirty miles per hour in a twenty-mile-per-hour-zone. I had not realized this before.

The line got shorter. As I overheard others discuss payments with the clerk, I silently hoped I had brought enough money. Being aware of the cost range, I had brought the maximum—$300.

Soon it was my turn. I walked to the window and presented my ticket to the attendant. She looked at it and said, "Would you like to make payment arrangements? Your ticket cost is $75." I couldn't believe my ears! I repeated it. "Seventy-five dollars?"

At that moment, I heard the Holy Spirit say "Acknowledge Me. Say "Thank you, Jesus." " I knew I needed to verbalize this and be obedient. "Thank you, Jesus! Praise the Lord!" I said. I then told the attendant I didn't need to set up a payment plan; I had enough money for the ticket.

On the way to the car, my sister and I could not stop talking about what God had done. "Thank you, Lord. Thank you, Jesus." With the rest of the money still in my hand, we talked about plans to spend the remaining $225. This was going to be fun.

Then something happened. A lady started running toward my sister and me. She waved her hands and shouted, "Oh, Miss! Oh, Miss!" We stopped as she approached. When she reached us, she said, "I've never done anything like this before, but I was in line back there, and I heard you acknowledge the Lord." She went on. "I don't have enough money to pay for my ticket, but I heard you acknowledge God. I'm from out of town, and I don't know when I could get back here to take care of this. Something told me to ask you if I could borrow the money."

Without hesitation, I asked her how much she needed. She said, "Two hundred and twenty-five dollars."

I had never put the money away. I replied, "You must be the reason this is still in my hand." It was the exact amount. I quickly gave it to her—a stranger—but she didn't seem like a stranger. I knew God had put her in my path.

She told us she was a Christian, and had she not heard me acknowledge God, she wouldn't have known where to turn. She took my name and address with promises of repayment. Whether she mailed the money or not was really of no concern to me. I was happy to be a blessing.

We didn't talk long. The office was closing, and she had to hurry inside to pay her bill. I was very excited! My bill was only $75, and I had money to give to someone in need.

Please do not misunderstand. I was not rich—not with monetary wealth. I was blessed with much more. I was available, obedient, and used by God. I have often heard people pray to God, asking for Him to go here or there—to bless this one or that one. The truth, however, is that we are to be the ambassadors for Christ, partaking in much of the work.

"Now then we are ambassadors for Christ, as though God did beseech you by us: we pray you in Christ's stead, be ye reconciled to God" (2 Corinthians 5:20, KJV).

We are to be the hands and feet of Jesus in today's world. I have chosen to avail myself to God.

"I beseech you therefore, brethren, by the mercies of God, that ye present your bodies as a living sacrifice, holy, acceptable unto God, which is your reasonable service" (Romans 12:1, KJV).

By week's end, I had received in the mail a check for $225 along with a beautiful, inspirational note of thanksgiving.

THE CLOCK

Sometimes getting myself and four young children ready for school was a little hectic, to say the least. Every morning was different. It seemed like there was always something added or forgotten.

I was repeatedly late for work—at least five to ten minutes just about every day. I was late enough for my superior to comment about my tardiness on more than one occasion. It didn't feel good, and I didn't understand why God allowed me to be consistently behind schedule. Why didn't He help me? I began to wonder who was letting who down. Was I letting God down? Was I a poor representative of Christ in my workplace?

Some say I am a perfectionist, but one thing people don't know is that we who are called perfectionists are oftentimes just people who like to follow the rules to the letter. If the time is 11:00, then 11:00 it is—not one minute before or after. In fact, I wouldn't even say that I am a perfectionist, but rather a person who wants to be like Christ and pleasing to God. Philippians 3:14 says, *"Do all things without murmurings and disputings"* (KJV).

One day, my boss was waiting for me as I walked in the door—yes, late again. He reprimanded me and said he would have to write me up if my tardiness continued. I tried to reach a sympathetic ear, hoping he might have pity on me and overlook it, but to no avail. He was, of course, justified in his actions. I had always adhered to a high standard, but my morning schedule just wasn't reaching the mark.

That night, as always, I planned everything. I got the diaper bags together and had everything packed for the next day. I went over in my head how the morning would play out. I planned to get to work on time every day, but it just wasn't happening. I did not plan for the spontaneous chaos or interruptions that seemed destined to occur.

It usually took me about forty minutes to get to work. This included dropping two children off at one school, where the kids were not allowed on campus until the bell rang, which was fifteen minutes before I had to be at work. The other two children went to a nursery two blocks from my office. Once I arrived at work, I had to park in the company's lot across the street from our building. Making all these stops and still walking into the office on time seemed like quite a feat. This routine, however—without interruptions or traffic jams—had gone smoothly in the past, even with ten minutes to spare.

The next morning, I pleaded to God, "Please help me get to work on time." As I drove my usual route, every traffic light seemed to have my name on it. "Please, God." My prayers continued. Time ticked away.

After dropping the babies off, my time had dwindled down to ten minutes. If I caught another red light, I'd be doomed—but I did, one light, and then another. "Please, God! Can you help me? Can you stop time? Please, God, I know you can do it! You can do anything you want, and I'll do anything you want me to do." I was desperate.

God knew I was a shy person, but that had never stopped me from ministering. One-on-one was the perfect setting for me. My coworkers all knew I was a child of the King. They often came to me for advice, knowing I would give them God's perspective through His Word.

So there I was, sitting at another red light, just across the street from the lot. I had five minutes left on the clock and a ten-minute destination. I was late. "Please, God, stop the clock for me! Let me get there on time."

As I pulled into a parking spot, I looked at the clock in the car. It read the same time as it had when I was at the light. He stopped the time; the

Lord had stopped the clock! I quickly walked to the corner but arrived just as the cross light changed to "don't walk."

When permitted, I crossed the street and hurriedly went up the stairs of the building. As I entered the door, I looked up at the clock. I was five minutes early. Praise the Lord! I was on time; Jesus had stopped the clock!

The Holy Spirit spoke to me. His instructions were to tell all of my coworkers, supervisors, and managers what had happened. I was to leave no one out. God wanted me to show my gratitude by openly giving Him praise and honor.

I was obedient. I immediately began going to each station, sharing how the Lord had blessed me by stopping time—how He had supplied my need. I told them I was going to be late again, but He stepped in and rescued me. I didn't speak softly, either. I was overjoyed.

Some believed my story and shared in my excitement, while others said my watch must have been wrong. It was up to them. They could believe or not, but I knew what God had done for me, and I told everyone.

"I will bless the Lord at all times: his praise shall continually be in my mouth" (Psalm 34:1b, KJV).

I realized, in fact, that I might have let God down, but He would never let me down. God wanted me to depend on Him for everything. The miracle God provided for me that morning not only reminded me of His goodness and continual presence, but also built my trust and increased my faith.

"There shall not any man be able to stand before thee all the days of thy life: as I was with Moses, so I will be with thee: I will not fail thee, nor forsake thee" (Joshua 1:5, KJV).

THE SUPERVISOR

One day, there was a need for a supervisor in my office. The company hired someone from the outside. The new supervisor came in on a Monday morning, and by lunch, made a lot of enemies. While being the new kid on the block must have been hard, she quickly changed many procedures. My coworkers and I all acknowledged that our once pleasant work environment was no more.

Dorothy was the supervisor's name, and she seemed to consistently display a bad attitude. She didn't greet us in the mornings or join our coffee break chats. All she seemed to want to do was be a bossy boss. Dorothy acted as if she did not like anyone. This was a new experience for me, as I couldn't remember ever encountering someone who didn't like me.

I began to pray for Dorothy every night. You know the prayer when we want God to fix someone: "Dear Lord, please help Dorothy." Then the Holy Spirit spoke to me. He reminded me of the Scripture in Proverbs 16:3 that says, *"Commit thy works unto the Lord, and thy thoughts shall be established"* (KJV). I asked the Holy Spirit to lead me, and He began to give me thoughts on how to proceed. The Spirit told me to begin by simply saying "Good morning" to Dorothy as she entered the room and to say her name.

The next morning, I greeted her. "Good morning, Dorothy."

Dorothy responded with "Good morning." There was no eye contact; she continued to walk straight to her desk.

After a few days, I added, "How are you today?"

"Fine, thank you," Dorothy answered. But still, there was no eye contact.

Then one day, it finally happened. I said, "Good morning, Dorothy. How are you?"

Dorothy responded with a smile. "Good morning, Peggy." Under my breath and with a sigh of relief, I said, "Thank you, Lord." My insides burst with joy. I knew that God could do anything, even melt a hardened heart. God had blessed us both. Dorothy, whom I had thought of as an enemy, told me good morning.

Proverbs 16:7 says, *"When a man's ways please the Lord, he maketh even his enemies to be at peace with him"* (KJV).

My dialog with Dorothy grew daily. She even began to come into my office and chat. One day, as I ate my lunch in the break room, Dorothy walked in. We had an entire thirty minutes to talk and get to know each other. I found out she was like many of us—a sensitive person who had been hurt in the past by cruel people. I responded by saying, "You have to pray for them." Our conversation continued about other things. Smiles and laughter filled the room. We connected. She realized my agenda was simply to be her friend.

You can tell a lot about a person when you look into his or her eyes. As time passed and Dorothy and I greeted each other with a hearty "Good morning," I could not only see who she was, but our spirits also bore witness with each other.

Dorothy and I started going to lunch together almost every day. She began to ask questions about my faith and my relationship with God. Of course, I told her how I had given my life to Christ at a young age and that I depended on Him for everything. She said she believed in God and Jesus but that her relationship was lacking. She eventually decided to go back to church and start reading her Bible again. Our times together were special. Dorothy received the words the Lord gave me to say to her. And I could see the manifestation in her interaction with the other employees, too.

The time then came when my maternity leave was about to start. Not sure if we would see each other again, Dorothy and I went to lunch for the last time. The Holy Spirit told me to share with Dorothy how He used me to soften her heart with His presence and His Word. I told her that I had prayed for her. I told her how God had given me instructions on how to help her. She smiled. At the end of the work day, we said "I love you" to each other, exchanged a big hug, and with tears in our eyes, said goodbye.

Today I pray that Dorothy has a strong relationship with God and that she remembers me and shares our story as part of her testimony, too.

"Be kindly affectioned one to another with brotherly love; in honour preferring one another" (Romans 12:10, KJV).

God chose me, and I availed myself to Him. Years ago, God revealed to me that in order for me to serve Him, I had to be obedient to His Word. I began to study the Scriptures, leaning on God's every word as He gave me instruction and guidance. He began using me to share His Word and His wealth with others. At work, home, or even the supermarket, God has always given me the opportunity to lift up the name of Jesus in word and deed.

The stories you have read are just a glimpse into my spiritual journey and the many instances where God manifested Himself to me and through me. I hope you cheered me on as you read while giving God all the praise and honor, for it was not I who gave freely, but Christ Jesus who lives inside of me. It was not I who showed love, but Jesus, and if it were not for Him, my parents would not have lived their lives as they did or taught me to love Him.

"Thanks be unto God for his unspeakable gift" (2 Corinthians 9:15, KJV).

The Lord Heals

by Jody Calandro Kaiser

Joseph Dominic Calandro was one of ten children of Sicilian immigrants settling as farmers in Ticfaw, Louisiana. Born in 1922, he was the youngest son. He made it through life as a content country boy. Attractive, with a muscular build, he became a high school football star and college recruit. But World War II called the boys to become men and "beat those Japs." After returning from serving in the Philippines, he settled in the city of Baton Rouge to work as a carpenter. The post-war boom provided much work for him. Later, he became a builder. Successful and handsome, he was thirty-two and single.

She was of Scotch-Irish descent—a common mixed breed with uncommon beauty. A redhead was a rare thing—especially one as sweet as Bettie. Her shy smile was perfect; her eyes were the bluest indigo. At twenty-one, she had a waist size to match her age. Joe's good looks and easy smile won her.

Bettie's Southern Baptist parents viewed this as an unsuitable courtship. They greeted Joe at the door with reasonable suspicion. Regardless, love swept her away. Before long, Joseph carried her over the threshold of a colonial ranch in the suburbs, circa 1955. Ten months later, my sister Cheryl was born. Daddy's gentle nature became proof that he would be a wonderful husband and father. He had gained my grandparents' approval.

Attempting to escape from a strict upbringing, Mom converted to Catholicism when she perceived she could drink and smoke and still get to heaven. Along with her newfound Catholic faith was an aversion to birth control. Eight kids were born in ten years, with a final midlife baby to come later. My parents had six girls first—Cheryl, Pam, Paula, Jody, Tracy and Marcie. The neighborhood cheered when the first boy, Joseph Jr. (or Joey), came along. Then another boy, Chris, joined the brood. Trailing behind seven years later, my baby sister, Angie, made an uneven nine.

Ours was a lively household. Four little girls in starched pinafore dresses rode tricycles that circled in the driveway. Later came more kids, and bikes with banana seats. The *vroom* of boys on peddled cars and army explosion sounds mingled with girlish squeals. Mom sewed playsuits and dance costumes while rump roast simmered on the stove.

Two sets of bunk beds were in most bedrooms. We added a den and a fifth bedroom to the house, creating a maze of rooms. Our laundry pile resembled the levee along the Mississippi River. A huge wicker basket for the warm, clean clothes often accommodated a sleeping child.

Neighborhood kids and bikes aplenty defined our landscape. Football games in the front yard were regular events, with the entire junior high cheerleading squad eating out of our spaghetti pot.

The blue and white station wagon was not large enough for us to travel together. So Daddy customized a motor home with a folding bed for each of us. My bed was a long piece of three-quarter-inch plywood suspended between the driver and passenger bucket seats. Momma coveted those rare times when only her children were with her, far away from the extra kids we attracted.

When Momma was pregnant with her ninth child we took the motor home to Disney World, staying in Fort Wilderness. As soon as we got the camper hooked up, Daddy handed each of us a $20 bill, and off we went for the day, leaving Momma and Daddy to savor some precious time alone.

Cheryl was seventeen and Chris was seven when Angie was born—a welcome shock. Grandchildren came in rapid succession just two years afterward. Weekends kept Daddy away as he worked hard as a real estate broker and developer.

With muscle cars and boyfriends swarming like mosquitoes, my mother shouldered a lot of the childrearing duties. We all had to pitch in and help around the house. But Momma was not a good delegator of chores, and they tended to all fall back on her. She felt overwhelmed, disillusioned, and resentful. Her small waist had gone many babies ago. Peanut butter and cheese puffs became her comfort. Her beautiful red hair didn't get fixed most days. With the demands of life, she seldom flashed her perfect smile. She craved to be taken care of instead of being the caretaker. She longed for the joy of her early married years. In self-pity, she whispered, "If I would get sick, maybe then Joe would appreciate me."

God, in His grace, saw Momma's tears. He sent others to reach out to her and once again restore her to right standing with her heavenly Father through forgiveness of sins and faith in Jesus Christ. She realized it was a closer relationship with God that would fill all her emptiness. Momma was born again. Marcie and Tracy watched in amazement as Momma danced around the house, doing chores. Music could be heard from the stereo as it played eight-track tapes of her favorite Christian artists.

The charismatic movement of the 70s was still thriving, and Momma wanted everything the Lord would give her. She became reacquainted with the Bible of her Baptist childhood, listening to radio preachers as she hummed gospel tunes. This strange and wonderful joy Momma found intrigued me. After I went to college, I also committed my life to the Lord. I received the baptism of the Holy Spirit with the gift of speaking in tongues. Daddy also found a need for a change in his life. He gave his heart to the Lord and began attending a full gospel church alongside Momma. They were nearly inseparable. Their newfound love of God and each other was obvious.

The years left Momma with layers of disappointment, but the joy of the Lord became her strength. With any crisis involving their family, Momma and Daddy were there with a fire hose. They were a team of experts on matters of the day-to-day. Car breakdowns, attending school sporting events, sewing of prom and bridesmaid dresses, births of grandchildren, financial bankruptcy, adult children marrying and divorcing, moving furniture, graduations, hospitalizations—our needs always came before theirs. Caring for both of her parents, and brother, before they died added to the mix of stress in Momma's life. She was physically strong; her steady and loyal nature kept her puttering along.

Never having much of a life outside of family, Momma began to find her fulfillment through church involvement. "Miss Bettie" became a beloved children's church teacher. Things were looking up, but her fears and insecurities clung like long evening shadows. Her late diagnosis was a result of this fear. Momma had not seen a doctor in the twenty-two years since Angie was born.

Momma felt a lump in her breast in February of 1995 but didn't tell anyone. With so many children and grandchildren, she always seemed to be called upon in each crisis. *It can wait,* she thought. Her worries turned to prayer, but she still concealed her secret until there was tremendous pain between her shoulder blades. Never one to be sick and lie down, she took Advil by the handful and carried on. Daddy noticed the deformity. Ignoring his worst fear, he shrugged it off. "Bettie, I guess we are just getting older."

In October, she told me, "Jody, I have a lump in my breast." She expected me to immediately speak faithful words to her, pray, and make it all better. She was disappointed by my response: "Momma, you need to see a doctor."

It was fall of 1995. Daddy and a few other sisters went with Momma to have a mammogram and sonogram. Momma wasn't comforted when extra technicians came to hover over the resulting pictures. Their faces of concern were aglow, illuminated by the grave images on the screen. Momma was instructed to go the next day to see a breast specialist and that the appointment had already been made.

I went with Momma and Daddy to the breast specialist visit. As Daddy parked the car, Momma and I sat in the waiting room, staring blankly at the TV. The world watched as the O. J. Simpson double murder trial was in full swing. It sickened me to see, for the hundredth time, the film footage of the white Bronco, surrounded by police cars, float down the California freeway. I could hardly bear the clamor of DNA results and blood-stained gloves. There were no sweet conversations to make—no pleasant words to bridge this dark moment.

I could see the doctor's feet under his desk, twisting as he gave the death sentence. "You have fourth stage metastasized breast cancer," the doctor said, along with a lot of other medical words that meant nothing to me. This wasn't easy for him to say, and it was impossible for us to hear.

Silence hung over us as we rode home. The car closed us in like a coffin. Dad dropped me off at my house less than a mile from theirs. As I got out of the car, the only consoling words I could manage were, "Momma, you are a candidate for a miracle." It seemed like a hollow thing to say, because it was in my head but not yet in my heart.

The tumor was large and had wrapped its evil tentacles around my mother's spine, squeezing her vitality. Never before had I seen my mother wince in pain. I saw this demon cancer choking strength from an otherwise strong woman. Diagnosed at the age of sixty-one, she and Daddy finally had their youngest child in college. After forty years of childrearing, they had looked forward to a new phase of life together.

After so many years of not asking much for herself, Momma lost touch with what she wanted. Passive by nature, she wasn't much of a fighter. With a crisis in her own body, Momma had to learn how to assert her will. She had no choice but to enlist herself into miracle boot camp.

We consulted with a few different oncologists and radiologists to determine her course of therapy. The doctors weren't very optimistic. With chemotherapy, she was projected to live two years—without it, maybe one. She reasoned that taking chemotherapy would "delay the inevitable" and didn't want to feel sick throughout treatment. Baldness, to her, would invite pity and scream of infirmity. Momma's beautiful red hair hadn't turned gray with age, but instead was a strawberry blonde streaked with auburn. She opted to have radiation treatments and take an oral anti-estrogen. She would think about undergoing more aggressive chemotherapy treatments later. In the meantime, she prescribed for herself a regimen of feasting on God's Word and prayer, with the intention of receiving a miraculous healing.

Growing in faith, my mother poured herself out before the Lord. For the first time in her life, she became consumed with her own needs. Momma only wanted to focus on the Lord Jesus healing her. My father, eight brothers and sisters, and numerous grandkids all rallied around her. Daddy encouraged her, saying, "Bettie, when you get healed, we are going to travel all over the country in the motor home so you can tell your story." She printed copies of healing Scriptures. She special-ordered several copies of Dottie Osteen's book, *Healed of Cancer.* Not usually one to take charge, she asked each of us to quote Scriptures daily on her behalf.

If asked what Scripture she was standing in faith on, my mother flawlessly quoted Isaiah 53:4–5: *"Surely he hath borne our griefs, and carried our sorrows: yet we did esteem him stricken, smitten of God, and afflicted. But he was wounded for our transgressions; he was bruised for our iniquities: the chastisement of our peace was upon him; and by his stripes we are healed"* (KJV).

The Lord blessed us with many who reached out and ministered to Momma during her battle. She made two trips to Oklahoma to Rhema Prayer and Healing Center. The school held weekly sessions year-round. Two classes a day offered teaching packed with healing Scripture. She got very close to Jesus, her Lord.

Our pastor, Brother Russell, was able to counsel Momma and uncover how she had opened the door for Satan to attack her health. He coached her to renounce what she had spoken to herself during a difficult time in life. She submitted to his guidance and truly believed God for a miracle.

Over the years, Daddy sold Christmas trees at his family's grocery store. Momma also worked there, making evergreen wreaths with holly sprigs she hand-cut from their yard. They often took a grandchild or two to play among the trees while they worked. The scent of Frazier fir and Scotch pine couldn't console Daddy. The Christmas of 1995 his sweet Bettie wouldn't be there with him.

God sent the pastor of Cheryl's church, Pastor Larry, to come buy a Christmas tree. Daddy recognized him and said, "Please pray for my wife, Bettie. She has cancer." As the tree was fastened onto his vehicle, Pastor Larry scribbled on a cardboard tag and handed it to Daddy. "Bettie, be encouraged!" He invited Momma to a pastoral staff prayer meeting and wrote down the specifics.

Cheryl and I accompanied Momma to the prayer meeting and quietly slipped into the back of the chapel. Pastor Larry motioned for us to come forward to the altar. God's presence was felt very strongly due to our own expectancy and the faith of the pastors there. Each of us fell backward as the pastors laid their hands on us and prayed. I lay beside Momma, unable to move physically. Within my spirit, I was moved with compassion as I heard Momma's hyena-like gasps of laughter mixed with groans of deliverance.

Radiation therapy had little ill effect on Momma. Deciding to go ahead and undergo chemotherapy, she drove herself to the first treatment. After the doctor examined her, he proclaimed that the tumors had shrunk and replied, "I see no need for you to have chemotherapy at this time." We all rejoiced. The whole family grew in faith that Momma would *"not die, but live, and declare the works of the Lord"* (Psalm 118:17, KJV).

We enjoyed several great times in 1995 and 1996. At the age of sixty-one, Momma saw a mountain for the first time. Shortly after, she took her first airplane ride. When the pilot heard of her, he invited her to sit in the cockpit for a photo.

On her birthday in May, several of us took Momma and Daddy to tour a plantation home. Ordinarily camera-shy, Momma posed with a smirk on her sweet face standing before the grand home. There were times that we almost forgot about the c-word.

As always, we spent most weekends at Momma and Daddy's house. Early in the fall of 1996 was the beginning of college football season. Thirteen grandchildren played all over the house and yard. The guys lounged in the den, watching a game on television, while the girls gathered around the large dining room table. As the girls laughed and talked about TV shows, hairstyles, and home decorating, Momma quietly slipped away and found an empty chair by the den window. She swiveled the chair to gaze outside, separating herself from anything that didn't focus on Jesus.

This detachment concerned me, and I mentioned it to her the next day.

She asked me, "Is it wrong to be uncaring about anything else but my healing?"

I replied, "No, Momma. That's not wrong." She cared less about the world around her. I wondered if Momma really did want to live or if she was just speaking in faith because it was the Christian thing to do.

Although a nagging pain developed in Momma's thigh, she refused to be issued a handicap license plate, not conceding to disease. My father, brothers, and sisters all pitched in and checked on Momma, helping with housework, cooking, doctors' appointments, and treatments for several months. She enjoyed our company more than she needed the help. Cheryl and I were there to visit and help Momma around the house from Monday through Friday. Pam and Paula took over on weekends, with Joey helping, too. Tracy's family lived a couple of hours away and came in town often. With a toddler and a second baby on the way, Marcie visited a lot. Angie was a senior in college, still living at home, helping mostly at night. Chris and his wife were expecting their first baby and lived in Dallas. They drove in whenever they could.

I was fortunate to visit with Momma almost every weekday afternoon. Together we'd pray, read the Bible, and chat about things. Being one of nine, I savored every ounce of time with my precious, godly mother. After thirty-six years, I finally had her all by myself. I wrapped her attention around me like hands cupped around a mug of fresh, hot coffee. Together we would sing favorite hymns from her Baptist childhood. We pulled out the hymnal from the piano bench and sang "Just a Closer Walk with Thee":

> Just a closer walk with Thee,
> Grant it, Jesus, is my plea,
> Daily walking close to Thee,
> Let it be, dear Lord, let it be.
>
> I am weak, but Thou art strong,
> Jesus, keep me from all wrong,
> I'll be satisfied as long
> As I walk, let me walk close to Thee.

Through this world of toil and snares,
If I falter, Lord, who cares?
Who with me my burden shares?
None but Thee, dear Lord, none but Thee.

We made it through the second and third verses. When we got to the fourth verse, her voice softened.

When my feeble life is o'er,
Time for me will be no more,
Guide me gently, safely o'er
To Thy kingdom's shore, to Thy shore.

Momma got choked up and could no longer sing. Momma was afraid to die.

"Jody, write a prayer for me using all the Scriptures that apply to my healing," she asked. "Then I can read it aloud and confess it. I just can't seem to concentrate enough to write it myself." Somehow, I never got around to it, which turned out to be the providence of God.

The cancer ate away at Momma's femur bone. Her characteristic waddle became a painful limp. Doctors performed surgery to insert a rod in her thigh for support when the bone inevitably broke. There were more setbacks. Scans showed spots on her ribs, brain, and liver. Nausea overwhelmed her. Our time together was often uncomfortable as she clutched a plastic bag, just in case. She physically could endure less activity. Our special visits were ending. When I arrived, I simply made her oatmeal, gave her anti-nausea medicine, and then cleaned house and prayed while she slept.

On a Friday in late October, Tracy and Daddy took Momma to the oncologist's office. The doctor asked her, "On a scale of one to ten, ten being the worst, how would you rate your pain?"

My mother responded, "A ten."

Typical of my mother—when the doctor left the room, she assured Tracy and Daddy, "Well, only when I walk, it's a ten. Otherwise, it's only a two or a three." The doctor, however, ordered medicine for a pain level of ten. At that point, he ordered hospice care alongside the controlled substance pain medicine, morphine. We naively understood hospice to be home health care and welcomed the idea. We did not know that hospice care typically meant "the end."

The following Sunday afternoon, the hospice home care nurse paid a visit. Momma sat in bed, sweetly conversing with the nurse. She felt that this was a nice gesture by nice people, and we would consider their services when the time came. No papers were signed. That evening, after she took the first morphine pain pill, she stumbled and fell on the way to the bathroom. Daddy called my husband, Jay, and I to come over and help lift her off the floor. With all of us taking turns bringing Momma to the doctor, it seemed the information didn't always pass on to the next caregiver in the family. We didn't realize how strong the medicine was.

Paula stayed at our parents' home Sunday night, and Daddy was with Momma all day Monday. In previous weeks, Cheryl and I alternated mornings and afternoons on weekdays. That morning, however, Cheryl called me from Momma's house and said, "Jody, this is minute-to-minute care. It will take two of us to care for her now."

Twelve hours prior to that call, Momma had taken the pain medication prescribed to her. When I arrived, she was sitting in a wheelchair, her head wobbling with drowsiness. Her speech was slurred, and she was vaguely cohesive. I asked her, "Momma, who's your healer?"

"Jesus," Momma said as she smiled weakly.

"Do you want us to pray for you and fight for your healing?" I asked.

Momma lazily nodded and slurred, "That's right. Amen."

Daddy left shortly after I arrived. He was overwhelmed and in need of a break. He went to lunch with a good friend. For the first time, I spoon-fed Momma oatmeal. She was too heavily medicated to feel humiliation. Cheryl and I decided that although it was time for the next pain pill dosage, the medicine was too strong, and she would not take it. I laid out her anti-nausea medicine and must have turned away. Momma took a pill from the morphine bottle, thinking it was the anti-nausea medicine. She may have taken one or more pills from the bottle. Realizing her error, we were exasperated. We had twelve more hours of Momma being incoherent.

Cheryl and I wheeled Momma to her bed and positioned her on her back, as she preferred. Realizing we needed more home care items to care for her, Cheryl made a quick run to the drug store.

I was alone with Momma. Quietly, I eased into the armchair in the corner of the bedroom. I had never watched my mother sleep before. In all those years of her tireless mothering, I couldn't recall ever seeing her rest. The sounds of her deep, rhythmic breaths filled the room. She was a very deep sleeper. Daddy envied that about her. He'd chuckle, "A tornado could come through the bedroom, and Bettie wouldn't wake up." As children, if we needed anything in the middle of the night, our insomniac father was the one who took care of us.

Deep in thought, I gazed at her, and then quietly prayed in tongues and in English. "Oh, Lord, help us through this time. Bring the manifestation of your healing power into her body. Oh, Lord Jesus, do a mighty work."

I watched Momma sleep as she lay on her back. She was really in a deep sleep, snoring like a locomotive train. I leaned forward in the chair, alarmed at the strange way her breath blew like a smoke stack. Her breathing became extremely labored; her ribcage visibly heaved as she struggled to get air. Then Momma's face had the look of fear, and I realized she was in trouble—perhaps slipping into a coma. I could feel a demonic presence hovering over the bed. The evil presence became visible to me. Its dark mass rapidly swooshed over her in a figure eight motion. I began to panic. I couldn't think of a Scripture. I began to cry aloud to God for help, and suddenly, God's Word came to me. I loudly quoted 2 Timothy 1:7: *"For God hath not given us the spirit of fear; but of power, and of love, and of a sound mind!"* (KJV)

The Holy Spirit rose within me, and I began to shout, "No, Devil!

You will not take my mother this way! This is not the way she'll die! I command you, spirit of death, to loose your hold on Momma and leave her in Jesus' name! No weapon formed against Momma will prevail." Thank God, after I warred in the spirit realm, the death angel left.

Once I felt I could safely leave the room, I went to the phone number list in the kitchen. I called Pam at work, explaining Momma's labored breathing. Pam said, "Get her upright! She needs oxygen!"

I hurried back into the bedroom and tried to pull Momma up by the arms, but she was too limp to cooperate. I ran to the den, grabbed all the cushions off the sofa, and lined them up against the bedside chest. In order to lift her by myself, I squeezed behind her, placing my back against hers. I pushed my legs against the wall, and as my back held her upright, I grabbed the sofa cushions beside the bed and propped her up with them, one cushion at a time. Easing myself out from behind her, I propped her arms up with several pillows to keep her from sliding. After she was more upright, her breathing seemed to become less strained.

I called Marcie, who had just had a baby, and asked her to get on the phone and order a hospital bed and oxygen. We had not signed for hospice care yet. All the paperwork needed to be done immediately in order to get any equipment delivered. Joey somehow got a bed delivered quickly. We pushed the queen-sized bed against the wall and moved the dresser over to make room for the oxygen machine.

That Tuesday night, as the effects of the narcotics wore off, our family gathered around Momma. Jay played the guitar, and we all sang worship songs and hymns. Momma's large family worshipping God together was like a dream to her. She sat up in bed and looked around the room. She raised her hands in praise and sang softly. Apparently very touched, she soaked it all in. "It's beautiful," she said as she smiled her perfect smile. Tracy and her family had recently moved away and were driving into town. Chris's family was also on its way. Friends from church held prayer meetings and provided practical service to the family of their much-loved Miss Bettie.

Later into the night, it seemed that Momma was only breathing as deeply as her throat; a rattling noise was heard with each breath. The hospice nurse said with her breathing pattern as shallow and raspy as it was, she may not make it through the night. Most of my brothers and sisters stayed at the house through the night, keeping vigil. We quietly prayed, sang, and offered her drinks through a straw. She didn't speak but was aware of our desire to be there for her and pray for her. We were on a life mission. I did not want to continue to give Momma the pain medicine. She isn't moaning or flinching with pain, I reasoned. The medicine caused us to lose communication with her, and I feared it caused her body to cooperate with death. My opinion was overruled, and we continued to administer the morphine every twelve hours.

Instead of sleeping heavily, Momma kept a fretful gaze, staring ahead. She would repeatedly raise her hand with a weak fist, seemingly a gesture of fear and desperation. Was this a nervous impulse, or was Momma trying to say something? Was this a sign of her fighting to live?

We were all a bit sleep-deprived. Taking my turn, I found a spare bed and tried to lie down and sleep, but my sister, Paula, woke me to ask, "Can you get up and pray your prayer language? Momma seems to be more at peace when you are praying with her." Even when I prayed, the stunned gaze or gesture with her fist didn't go away.

The next day, Wednesday, the hospice staff advised us to get funeral plans in order and let Momma go. I dealt very little with the hospice nurses. Other sisters handled all of that. The nurses were kind and caring people, but I hardly could leave Momma's side. I held to my stance that the fight wasn't over. I didn't want to make funeral arrangements.

That afternoon we gathered around the dining room table. Most of the family was leaning toward letting her go, yet I couldn't. I said, "Momma told me to fight for her and believe for her healing, and that is what I am going to do." Oddly, I began to laugh and lay my head on the table, partly crying. The weeping turned to laughter, and then laughter became crying again. *Okay*, I thought, *nights and days of no sleep and non-stop prayer are making me loony.*

I suddenly realized that although Momma was no longer speaking, she was still conscious, and we could communicate like I had seen in old movies. "She can squeeze my hand!" I jumped up from the table and rushed beside her bed with a few of my sisters and brothers following. I said, "Momma, this is Jody. If you know this is Jody, then squeeze my hand." She squeezed my hand. I then said, "Momma, I am going to ask you two questions. You answer me 'yes' by squeezing my hand. First, I will ask you if you want to go be with the Lord. Then, I'll ask you if you want us to fight for you and believe God for your healing." I asked, "Okay, do you want to go be with the Lord?" I felt no squeeze. I then asked, "Do you want us to fight for you and believe God for a miracle?" Not only did she squeeze my hand, but she also raised my hand up in the air. It was clear to all of us what she wanted.

By that time, it was Wednesday night. As 2 Corinthians 10:4 states, *"The weapons we fight with are not the weapons of the world. On the contrary, they have divine power to demolish strongholds."*

It was spiritual warfare time—time for God's healing power to transform my mother's body. Those who wanted to stay and pray did. Those who chose to leave the room left. Shortly afterward, Brother Russell arrived, and we began a new level of intercession.

The day before, we had moved Momma's Bible and notebooks aside to make room for the hospital bed and oxygen machine. Imagine—the living Word of God that Momma so desperately needed had been pushed aside! Tucked inside her Bible, we found a treasure of healing Scriptures, notations, Scripture cards, and pamphlets that she had treasured and claimed. Her Bible was worn, earmarked, highlighted, and underlined. The Scriptures weren't just words on a page, but living in Momma's spirit! Tracy found the confession prayer of healing my mother had written. This was the prayer she had asked me to write, but thank God, she wrote it herself.

The presence of God became tangible as Tracy loudly read Momma's prayer. "I speak to my liver and command it to be free of cancer. I speak to my brain and command cancer to go from me in Jesus' name. He was wounded for my transgressions and bruised for my iniquities, and by Jesus' stripes, I am healed!" We knew her heart! We prayed when she could no longer pray.

A burden of intersession came on me as I stood in the gap for Momma. As Romans 8:26–27 explains, *"In the same way, the Spirit helps us in our weakness. We do not know what we ought to pray for, but the Spirit himself intercedes for us with groans that words cannot express. And he who searches our hearts knows the mind of the Spirit, because the Spirit intercedes for the saints in accordance with God's will."*

I began to wail and travail as never before. In our prayers, I felt the demonic stronghold flee at our commands in Jesus' name. A foul spirit of infirmity left Momma's body. I felt it leave my body also, its talons clutching inside my chest. Momma's breathing became normal and was no longer shallow. The death rattle gasping stopped. Her coloring went from a pasty yellow to a healthy pink. The swollen lymph edema in her left arm slowly deflated. She was healed.

Members of my family were in and out of the master bedroom and praying all over the house. Yet the most intense warfare was done in the master bedroom. I sensed there was more deliverance to come. It was the spirit of fear. It was a cowardly, insecure fear. It wasn't as big as the spirit of infirmity, but it was the demon that held my mother captive for so many years. We began to pray against that thing, and I quoted a Scripture aloud. *"For God hath not given us the spirit of fear; but of power, and of love, and of a sound mind!"* (2 Timothy 1:7, KJV) That was the verse that helped me through the trauma when the death angel was hovering over Momma the day before.

Pam said, "No, that's not it! That's not the Scripture! It's 'perfect love cast out fear,'" She quoted from 1 John 4:18, *"There is no fear in love. But perfect love drives out fear, because fear has to do with punishment. The one who fears is not made perfect in love."*

Pam began to describe perfect love. "Perfect love is God's love for us. He gave his Son, Jesus, to die for our sins. Perfect love is demonstrated by Jesus' work on the cross. Perfect love is the crown of thorns, the nail-scarred hands, and the spear in his side. By the lashes to Jesus' back,

Momma is healed." We thanked Jesus for his suffering for Momma's healing and kept praying.

Brother Russell sat in the chair in the corner with one hand holding his forehead. Tracy sat still, leaning against the wall by Momma's head. I paced in the small space between the bathroom and the feet of both beds. Pam rocked quietly in a chair squeezed between the two beds, stroking Momma's right hand. Pam kept her head down, wept softly, and asked God to rock Momma like a baby and comfort her. The peace of the Lord replaced the fear.

The aura of God's presence enfolded each of us in the room. From the direction of the bathroom came a bright light that was brighter than any day could give. I felt the warmth of its radiance, and with the force of an undertow, I was pulled to the floor. Brother Russell slumped in the chair from the unseen power. Pam saw, in the corner of her eye, Jesus walk from the bathroom, stepping over me to the opposite side of Momma's bed. Without daring to look up, she saw His nail-scarred hands and a golden sash around His waist. Jesus held Momma's left hand as He stood by the bed. Momma sat up in bed as Jesus talked to her. The room was quiet and peaceful for a long time. Only the sound of the oxygen machine lingered, as we all were unable to move. The work was done. She was free.

The silence was broken as Pam quietly wept, holding Momma's hand. I slowly got myself up from the floor as I heard her say, "Momma, I love you, and I will miss you. But if you want to go be with Jesus, then that would be okay. We will be fine, and we will take care of Daddy."

We had prayed through the crisis. My mother was delivered from the bondage of a spirit of infirmity and a spirit of fear. I fully expected Momma to get up and ask for oatmeal.

It was close to 3:00 Thursday morning. Brother Russell, sensing that the Lord had completed the work, got up and went to say goodbye to Miss Bettie. I heard him say, "I command you to breathe in Jesus' name." She took in a gasp of air. He said it again, and she took another breath. Daddy, Chris, and Angie rushed in. We all waited, surrounding her as she took a few more deep breaths. "She is making up her mind," someone said. No more breaths—she was in heaven. We looked at Daddy and waited for our cue. "I've got peace," he sighed. We all felt it, too. I reached out my hand and closed her beautiful blue eyes, which were still fixed on Jesus.

I did not have a trace of doubt that my mother had been healed. During the months following, however, I had a few questions for the Lord. Why was there so much effort for my mother to receive her miracle and then to die in the end? Why did she choose to be with Jesus? If she had taken chemotherapy, would we have had more time for her to be healed and live? The answers trickled down in various forms. The most assuring answer was found in Philippians 4:7: "*And the peace of God, which transcends all understanding, will guard your hearts and minds in Christ Jesus.*" I know that peace.

For months following Momma's healing, the Lord poured out His Spirit on me so strongly that I seemed to be walking in another realm. The most difficult time of my life had the most profound impact on it. I learned the power of believing God's Word. I understood the reality of having the faith to move the mountain of cancer. I had been delivered, too.

My mother wanted to be a victorious saint, and she was. She didn't want to die of cancer, and she didn't. She wanted to prove God's Word is true, and it is. She was healed completely and could have lived. God did not send His angels to touch her; Jesus Himself came to her side and gave His beloved saint the choice. And she chose to be with Him. The Lord heals.

Afterword

Backyard Miracles was composed to testify of God's faithfulness and glorify the Lord Jesus Christ. Our desire is that all who read this will know the love of the Father and the salvation that Christ offers to anyone who seeks Him.

"For God so loved the world that he gave his one and only Son, that whoever believes in him shall not perish but have eternal life" (John 3:16).

When you read this book, did you feel a tugging on your heart? Did you question if Jesus could be that real in your life? The great news is that He can!

Jesus is ready to come into your heart. He is waiting for you to invite Him. He wants to have a relationship with you, but He will not force you—it must be your personal decision. Think about your life and all the times He may have been gently speaking to you—through a song, a friend, a gentle breeze, a smile from a stranger, or an e-mail at just the right time. His ways are limitless and much higher than our own.

"When Jesus spoke again to the people, he said, 'I am the light of the world. Whoever follows me will never walk in darkness, but will have the light of life'" (John 8:12).

God is good, and He will demonstrate how much He adores you by bringing people and things, including this book, into your life to minister to you and show you His great love. Jesus wants to give you hope, joy, love, peace, and salvation. He wants you to have all these things and more.

"The thief comes only to steal and kill and destroy; I have come that they may have life, and have it to the full" (John 10:10).

Are you ready to receive Jesus—to welcome Him into your life? Yes?

Then let's pray:

> Father God, I thank You for sending Your only son, Jesus, born of a virgin, into this world to save me. Thank You that Jesus paid the ultimate price, His life, so that I may be forgiven. Thank You that His life was sacrificed on the cross for me—for the debt of all my sin and shame. He suffered that I may have life. The spotless Lamb of God died in my place! His death redeemed me, and He rose in victory three days later. He sits at Your right hand now, Father, and will return again one day.
>
> Jesus, thank You for living the life I couldn't, and thank You for giving up Your life so that I may live. Please forgive all my sins and wash me in Your blood so that I may be white as snow and acceptable to the Father.
>
> Holy Spirit, please make Yourself real to me. I want to experience Your love, peace, and joy. I ask You to help me read Your Word, the Bible, every day and to find a holy, Bible-based church home with strong Christian friends.
>
> Jesus, I ask that today You write my name in the Lamb's Book of Life. Let heaven keep this record. Lord, help me to serve You for the rest of my life. Give me the strength to walk this path with You, holding my hand. I thank You for Your unending love.
>
> Amen.

Today, I give my life to the Lord Jesus Christ.

_____

Name   Date

Authors

Emily Billings

Karen Carlino

Jessica Dupuy

Carrie Feder

Jeanine Garcia

Sharon Holeman

Authors

Joanna Jacob

Jody Calandro Kaiser

Sandra Mizell

Brandi Redmon

Peggy Taylor

Lori Wilkins

Resources

The Straightened Path—Karen Carlino

For more information on organ donation, visit the National Kidney Foundation at *kidney.org* or the Louisiana Organ Procurement Agency at *lopa.org*. Contact your nearest hospital for local information and assistance.

Sacrificing Isaac—Emily Billings

For more information on the internship program Emily participated in, contact Joyce Meyer Ministries. *joycemeyer.org*

Uprooted and In a Wilderness—Sandra Mizell

A resource similar to the private teaching Sandra and Garlin received can be found through Loving and Caring Inc. Ask for the Biblical Personality Profile System. *landcresources.org*

Other publications by Sandra Mizell include: *Live! You Didn't Die!* and *The Biggest and Best Trip Ever. sandramizell.com*

CPSIA information can be obtained at www.ICGtesting.com
Printed in the USA
LVOW052001120912

298489LV00003B/1/P